ACADEMIC ADVISING

Recent Titles in
Bibliographies and Indexes in Education

Integrating Women's Studies into the Curriculum: An Annotated Bibliography
Susan Douglas Franzosa and Karen A. Mazza, compilers

Teacher Evaluation and Merit Pay: An Annotated Bibliography
Elizabeth Lueder Karnes and Donald D. Black, compilers

The Education of Poor and Minority Children: A World Bibliography, Supplement, 1979–1985
Meyer Weinberg, compiler

Comparative Reading: An International Bibliography
John Hladczuk and William Eller, compilers

Higher Education in American Life, 1636–1986: A Bibliography of Dissertations and Theses
Arthur P. Young, compiler

Literacy/Illiteracy in the World: A Bibliography
John Hladczuk, William Eller, and Sharon Hladczuk, compilers

Career Index: A Selective Bibliography for Elementary Schools
Gretchen S. Baldauf, compiler

Institutions of Higher Education: An International Bibliography
Linda Sparks, compiler

General Issues in Literacy/Illiteracy: A Bibliography
John Hladczuk, William Eller, and Sharon Hladczuk, compilers

The American College President, 1636–1989: A Critical Review and Bibliography
Ann H. L. Sontz

College Admissions: A Selected, Annotated Bibliography
Linda Sparks, compiler

American Higher Education: A Guide to Reference Sources
Peter P. Olevnik, Betty W. Chan, Sarah Hammond, and Gregory M. Toth, compilers

Writing Across the Curriculum: An Annotated Bibliography
Chris M. Anson, John E. Schwiebert, and Michael M. Williamson, compilers

ACADEMIC ADVISING
An Annotated Bibliography

Compiled by
Virginia N. Gordon

Bibliographies and Indexes in Education, Number 14

GREENWOOD PRESS
Westport, Connecticut • London

Library of Congress Cataloging-in-Publication Data

Gordon, Virginia N.
    Academic advising : an annotated bibliography / compiled by
Virginia N. Gordon.
        p.   cm.—(Bibliographies and indexes in education, ISSN
0742–6917 ; no. 14)
    Includes bibliographical references and indexes.
    ISBN 0–313–28843–7 (alk. paper)
    1. Counseling in higher education—Bibliography.   I. Title.
II. Series.
Z5814.C83G67   1994
[LB2343]
016.3781'94—dc20   94–2865

British Library Cataloguing in Publication Data is available.

Library of Congress Catalog Card Number: 94–2865
ISBN: 0–313–28843–7
ISSN: 0742–6917

First published in 1994

Greenwood Press, 88 Post Road West, Westport, CT 06881
An imprint of Greenwood Publishing Group, Inc.

Printed in the United States of America

The paper used in this book complies with the
Permanent Paper Standard issued by the National
Information Standards Organization (Z39.48–1984).

10 9 8 7 6 5 4 3 2 1

Contents

Preface

This collection of annotated bibliographies represents an overview of the many and varied topics associated with academic advising. Included are 351 citations contained within ten topical areas found in advising and its related literature.

Although this directory only touches upon a small part of the vast amount of information on academic advising, it can act as a general guide to the recent publications on the subject. Since advising encompasses such a large area of institutional and student life, citations from the literature on related topics are included as well.

While some older classic articles and books associated with the field are mentioned, most of the citations are from the decades of the 1980s and 1990s. The topics were chosen so that researchers and practitioners could examine the literature based on their interest and need. For example, administrators concerned with improving their overall advising services might benefit from what is written about organizational and delivery systems. The two sections on special populations and minorities include helpful information about

the unique characteristics of these specific
groups. Citations outlining special
administrative approaches for these populations
are also included.

   Each section's citations are listed by the
first authors' name in alphabetical order. All
entries are numbered from the beginning to the
end of the book to faciltiate easy access and
identification.

Introduction

Academic advising has played an important role
in higher education since the time of the
colonial colleges. Although still perceived as
the purview of academic faculty, it's function
and scope have broadened considerably.
Advising is no longer viewed only as "course
scheduling." The complexity of curricula,
students' concerns about the competiveness of
the market place, and the changing nature of
the student population have made advising one
of the most important functions on campus.

Literature on the subject has exploded in
the past two decades. Not only have the many
research studies and "think-pieces" on
advising proliferated, but the information in
related fields has expanded as well. When
examining the many facets of advising, one has
only to look at the literature in other fields
(e.g., student development, psychology,
sociology, decision making, higher education,
retention, disabled students) to see how this
knowledge can be applied directly or indirectly
to the advising function. Since there is no
paucity of literature in the field, it was
difficult to narrow the scope of articles,
books and other published resources to the

confines of these pages.

Because of limited space, the annotations selected for this bibliography are primarily from the 1980s and 1990s. A few classic articles and books are included to give the subject a historical perspective.

The first chapter summarizes the literature on the topic of organizational and delivery systems. Since there is an abundance of information relating directly to advising in this area, this section is the largest. Chapter 2 gives an overview of developmental advising, which some may consider a type of delivery mode as well.

Chapter 3 is organized around the special types of students who advisers encounter. Adults, athletes, commuters, those with high-abilities, and those undecided are a few examples of students with special needs.

Chapter 4 offers citations dealing with another special group - those from culturally diverse backgrounds. Understanding the special histories and cultural differences of these students has become an critical aspect of advising. The need for advisers to be sensitive to their special needs is increasingly being recognized.

Adviser training has become an important part of delivering effective advising services since both faculty and professional advisers are in constant need of updating and expanding their knowledge and skills. Chapter 5 provides an overview of the literature in this area. Career advising (Chapter 6) has also become necessary in recent years since many students choose their academic majors based on career relationships. Many advisers are becoming more aware of the importance of understanding how vocational as well as academic decisions are made.

Academic advising has been emphasized as having a direct tie to student retention, so some of the studies outlining these relationships are contained in Chapter 7.

Citations dealing with legal issues in advising are covered in Chapter 8 since this area has recently emerged as one critical to advising practices. Viewing advising as a profession is another new area in the literature. Chapter 9 summarizes some of what has been written on this topic.

Finally, Chapter 10 provides an overview of the important publications on evaluation and assessment. The books that have been written about academic advising in general are listed in Chapter 11.

This bibliography has been compiled as a handy reference for faculty advisers, administrators, professional advisers, students, and anyone interested in examining the literature about academic advising and its many related topics. It will also serve those who wish to review the current literature as a basis for future research and study.

ACADEMIC ADVISING

Chapter 1

Organizational and Delivery Systems

A. General Approaches

1.   Backhus, D. (1989). Centralized
intrusive advising and undergraduate
retention. NACADA Journal, 9, 39-45.

A description of an undergraduate advising
center's practices in intrusive academic
advising is given. Intrusive advising refers
to the provision of advising whether or not a
student actively seeks it. Comparison of
enrollment before the implementation of the
program and after the implementation of
intrusive advising is given. Results
indicated that the four-year retention rate
increased from 31 percent to almost 40 percent
after the use of the program.

2.   Council for the Advancement of
Standards for Student Services/Development
Programs. (1986). Iowa City, IA: The
American College Testing Program.

Standards and guidelines for academic advising
are provided including mission, program,
organization and administration, human
resources, funding, facilities, campus and
community, relations, and ethics. The

standards and guidelines are prepared by the
Council for the Advancement of Standards
(CAS).

3.   Crookston, B.B. (1972). A developmental
view of academic advising as teaching. Journal
of College Student Personnel, 13, 12-17.

In this classic article, Crookston seeks to
individualize academic advising by describing
two models of advising: a prescriptive
approach and a student development approach.
Prescriptive advisers are characterized as
authoritarian and assume responsibility for
students' progress. A developmental adviser
assumes a more holistic approach and shares
responsibility with students for their
adjustment and progression through college in
academic, social and vocational areas. The
adviser assumes a teaching role in the
advising exchange and respects the uniqueness
of each student being advised.

4.   Frank, C.P. (1988). The development of
academic advising programs: Formulating a
valid model. NACADA Journal, 8, 11-28.

A nationwide survey was conducted to test the
validity of a theoretical model of advising
program development. Respondents generally
supported the Four Stage Model, which outlined
the direction, nature and scope of changes
leading toward an effective advising service.
However, the survey revealed disagreement on
the stimulus/response relationship outlined in
the model, the component of each stage, and
the amount of overlap among stages. The model
was the adjusted to depict more accurately the
sequence of changes common to most advisement
programs. The revised model provided advising
and administration with a framework for
understanding the process of development and a
basis for planning program improvements.

5.   Gordon, V.N. (1992). Delivering academic advising services. In V. Gordon, Handbook of Academic Advising, (pp. 21-46). Westport, CT: Greenwood Press.

The chapter is organized around the building blocks of academic advising including the why, what, who, where, when and how of delivering advising services. Student, adviser and institutional needs are discussed. The many functions associated with advising are detailed. Organizational configurations are outlined and the types of advisers are described. Many other aspects of providing a comprehensive program are included.

6.   Habley, W.R. (1983). Organizational structures for academic advising. Journal of College Student Personnel, 24, 535-540.

This article presents seven existing organizational structures for academic advising and enumerates several practical concerns that must be addressed before implementing an organizational structure. The seven organizational models for advising are described in detail and ten practical implications are presented to provide a framework for research on the effectiveness of each of the models.

7.   Habley, W.R. (1993). Fulfilling the promise? ACT fourth national survey on academic advising. Iowa City, IA: American College Testing Program.

This report presents the final results of the 4th National Survey of Academic Advising. Over 400 institutions responded to questions about coordination and organization of campus advising practices, delivery of advising services, overall goal and achievement, and institutional effectiveness. Some conclusions are that advising offices are severely

overloaded, and while improvement in advising
is seen in many areas, adviser/advisee ratios
and time spent in advising have remained
unimproved. Four year colleges are lagging
behind in advising practices when compared to
other types of institutions. The achievement
of developmental goals for academic advising
programs is still far from satisfactory.
There have been important gains in the
perceived effectiveness of advising programs,
however. There is also increasing diversity
in the type of people who are providing
advising.

8.   Habley, W.R. (1993). The organization
and effectiveness of academic advising in
community colleges. In M.C. King (Ed.),
Academic advising: Organizing and delivering
services for student success, New Directions
for Community Colleges, No. 82. San
Francisco: Jossey-Bass.

This chapter details the results of the
American College Testing Program's fourth
national survey as it pertains to community
colleges. Organizational models,
institutional policies, adviser training,
evaluation and program goals are summarized.

9.   Hazelton, V., & Tuttle, G.E. (1981).
Performance appraisal: A new model for
academic advisement. Journal of College
Student Personnel, 22, 213-218.

The performance appraisal model for student
advisement is examined. This model is a
centralized developmental model that focuses
on the content and process of advisement. The
model's content is discussed through
objectives and job definitions, including
performance assessment and goal setting.
Operation of the model is described. Four
benefits and two patented limitations of the
model are identified.

10.   Iaccino, J. (1987). Developing an effective delivery system: The Freshman Advising Program. NACADA Journal, 7, 41-42.

Advising is discussed as a key to students' survival and success in college. The Freshman Advising Program, created to improve the status and activity of advising in one educational institution, is described. The overall results of the program have been positive. The major finding was that freshmen felt their adviser had helped them formulate tentative objectives for college, and assisted them in selecting appropriate courses consistent with their career plans.

11.   King, M.C. (1993). Advising models and delivery systems. In M.C. King (Ed.), Academic advising: Organizing and delivering services for student success, New Directions for Community Colleges, No. 82. (pp. 47-54) San Francisco: Jossey-Bass.

This is a review and discussion of seven organizational models of academic advising and five delivery systems. An ideal advising model and delivery system for community colleges is offered.

12.   O'Banion, T. (1972). An academic advising model. Junior College Journal, 42, 62-69.

Many community college educators feel that a different academic advising model may be more appropriate for the community colleges and their students. This article proposes a model based on a logical sequence of steps to be following in the process of academic advising. The model, while geared to the community college, would probably be adaptable to four-year colleges and universities as well.

13.   Spicuzza, F.J. (1992). A customer

service approach to advising: Theory and
application. <u>NACADA</u> <u>Journal,</u> <u>12,</u> 49-58.

The author describes a customer service
marketing model to provide an organizing
strategy for academic advising in higher
education. According to this model, customers
are the focal point and the reason for the
organization's existence. Six key ingredients
are outlined: a) customer needs, b) employee
attitude, c) administrative commitment, d)
training and resources, e) recognition, and f)
evaluation. Each of these six ingredients are
described. With a customer service approach,
everyone benefits - the university, the
academic programs, the faculty and the
students.

14.   Wilder, J.R. (1981). A successful
academic advising program: Essential
ingredients. <u>Journal</u> <u>of</u> <u>College</u> <u>Student</u>
<u>Personnel,</u> <u>22,</u> 488-492.

The author advocates academic advising
programs which center on four basic
ingredients: selection, training, evaluation,
and recognition of advisers. When combined
with adequate numbers of advisers, good
referral agencies, sufficient clerical help,
and cooperation with other segments of the
university, advising programs can adequately
service the student population. Strategies
for the four basic ingredients are discussed.

B. **Faculty Advising**

15.   Beasley-Fielstein, L. (1986). Student
perceptions of the developmental advisor-
advisee relationship. <u>NACADA</u> <u>Journal,</u> <u>6,</u> 107-
117.

The quality of the student-faculty interaction
in academic advising is a major contributing
variable to institutional holding power.

Students were surveyed for the type of relationship that was most productive, qualitative, and satisfying for them. Student development theory in advising was explored.

16.   Borgard, J.H., Hornbuckle, P.A., & Mahoney, J. (1977). Faculty perceptions of academic advising. NASPA Journal, 14, 4-10.

Faculty attitudes toward academic advising were examined. Faculty were asked for their views of the need for advising, its professional relevance, and student faculty involvement.

17.   Dehn, S. (1987). Using faculty to advise new students. NACADA Journal, 7, 62-66.

In an effort to improve certain critical areas in the academic advising system, faculty and administrators at St. Joseph's college developed an advising approach using a team of faculty advisers from different disciplines to advise all incoming students. A description of the "new strategy" and its results appear in this article.

18.   Dressel, F.B. (1974). The faculty adviser. Improving College and University Teaching, 22, 57-58.

This article discusses the functions and opportunities of the faculty adviser. Suggestions for utilizing professional academic advisers within each college or school are also explored.

19.   Fielstein, L.L. (1987). Student preferences for personal contact in a student-faculty advising relationship. NACADA Journal, 7, 34-40.

A study to "arrive at a clearer understanding

of the type of relationship students want when
interacting with a faculty adviser" is
described. The results indicate that most
students think it is important for their
adviser to be personally acquainted with them.

20.   Hardee, M.D. (1970). Faculty advising
in colleges and universities. Student
Personnel Series Monograph No. 9, American
College Personnel Association.

This monograph describes the practice of
faculty advising in higher education as based
on a philosophical and psychological base of
advising as constructed by Lewis B. Mayhew,
Professor of Higher Education, Stanford
University. First, the needs of and problems
faced by the undergraduate student are
described. The college environment between
the teacher and the learner are outlined.
Intent and scope of faculty advising are
explained. The monograph ends by describing
adviser preparation and program evaluation
strategies and by looking ahead at the future.

21.   Hornbuckle, P., Mahoney, J., &
Borgard, J.H. (1979). A structural analysis
of student perceptions of faculty advising.
Journal of College Student Personnel, 20, 296-
300.

This article describes a study of students'
perceptions of the faculty advising process.
Perceptions were found to be relatively
undifferentiated, emphasizing students'
reactions to perceived social skills of
advisers, with minimum awareness of technical
functions. Other findings and implications
for training and evaluation of advisers are
discussed.

22.   Kramer, G.L., et al. (1985). The
academic advising center and faculty advising:
A comparison. NASPA Journal, 23, 24-35.

This article assesses the perceptions of
students, faculty, and administrators of the
role and success of academic advising centers
and faculty advisers. Results indicated
significant differences in perceptions across
groups.

23.   Kramer, H.C. (1983). Advising:
Implications for faculty development. <u>NACADA</u>
<u>Journal, 3,</u> 25-31.

A healthy advising program serves as a useful
vehicle for faculty development. An
institution may use the program to develop
faculty skills useful in other contexts than
the individual student's welfare. Advising
programs should endeavor to improve students,
faculty, and the institution.

24.   Kramer, H.C., & Gardner, R.E. (1983).
<u>Advising</u> <u>by</u> <u>faculty</u> (rev.ed.). Washington,
D.C.: National Education Association. (ERIC
Document Reproduction Service No. 235 742)

A guide for faculty advisers is presented that
addresses aspects of the advising process that
are often not discussed. Objectives are to
provide a working definition and theoretical
framework for advising and to provide
procedures for adviser self-evaluation.
Additional topics include: the faculty
advising contract, the use of a visual model
for planning, effective communication and
risk-taking, and informational advising.

25.   Lumpkins, B., & Hall, H. (1987).
Advising college undergraduates: A neglected
art. <u>College</u> <u>Student</u> <u>Journal, 21,</u> 98-100.

Consistent and proper advisement of
undergraduate college students has been found
to be a major determinant of college
retention. The purpose of the paper is to
review research relative to advising and to

propose measures for improving the advising
process. A major fault with the advising
process appears to center around the lack of
training and preparation of college professors
to serve as advisers. These skills which
relate to the counseling field seem to be also
essential for academic advising.

26.   McAnulty, B.H., O'Connor, C.A., &
Sklare, L. (1987). Analysis of student and
faculty opinion of academic advising services.
NACADA Journal, 7, 49-61.

As college student enrollment continues to
decline on regional and national levels,
faculty members and administrators are
increasingly concerned about the corresponding
loss of revenue. Closely aligned with this
concern, and also with the increased intensity
of recruitment activities, is the emphasis on
retention. At the same time, the quality of
academic advising provided to an institution's
students is being carefully scrutinized,
particularly for its relationship to
retention. This article reports on the
results of a questionnaire dealing with
faculty and student perceptions of the role of
advising and the adviser in academic
institutions.

27. Stokes, J.P. (1992). Evaluation of a
pilot program of faculty advising at an urban
commuter university. NACADA Journal, 12, 28-
33.

This study manipulated informal contact with
faculty by assigning students to a faculty
adviser as part of a pilot project. A control
group with no faculty assignment was also
established. The purpose of the study was to
determine the effect of faculty contact and
advising on retention and on intervening
variables such as satisfaction with college or
academic achievement. Only 13% of the

students assigned a faculty adviser made contact with them. The most common reason reported for not making contact was that students were too busy. In the authors' opinion, the lack of a cohesive campus community is an obstacle to implementing faculty advising. Comparing the students who did see an adviser with the control group revealed no significant differences on outcome measures. In spite of the lack of student interest, the authors are convinced that faculty contact can be useful in establishing a more hospitable learning environment.

28.   Teague, G.V., & Grites, T.J. (1980). Faculty contracts and academic advising. Journal of College Student Personnel, 41, 40-44.

This article describes a study which investigated the degree to which academic advising is described as an official faculty responsibility by examining current collective bargaining agreements and institutional documents. The findings suggested specification of duties required of faculty advisers is generally neglected in all forms of agreements, regardless of the kind of institution. Other findings and implications are described.

29.   Trombley, T.B. (1984). An analysis of the complexity of academic advising tasks. Journal of College Student Personnel, 25, 234-239.

This study analyzed the tasks of faculty advisers in a survey of 925 college students who rated the importance of the tasks and their adviser's performance. Factor analysis provided confirmation for dichotomizing tasks according to their level of complexity and type of skill.

30.   Vowell, F., & Karst, R. (1988).
Student satisfaction with faculty advisors in
an intrusive advising program. NACADA
Journal, 7, 31-33.

This is a description of an instrusive faculty
advising system which serves all freshmen and
undeclared students. A questionnaire was
developed to gather information of students'
perceptions of their faculty advisers and the
Student Advising Office. Levels of
satisfaction were quite high and this is
attributed to the intrusive nature of the
advising approach.

31.   Weaver, F.S. (1987). Academic
advising as teaching. Innovative Higher
Education, 12, 22-25.

Faculty-led advising seminars for advisees are
recommended as a way to increase the
effectiveness of the academic advising system.
Through the seminars, the advising function
would be integrated into the course-credit
system and provide students with opportunities
to systematically reflect on the nature of
higher education.

C.   Departmental Advising

32.   Cremer, C.V., & Ryan, M. (1984).   New
techniques let students evaluate academic
advising. Journalism Educator, 39, 21-22.

This article describes the questionnaire
developed to measure student perceptions of
the quality of academic advising they
received. Competed questionnaires were
analyzed and a summary was presented to all
faculty members in the School of Journalism.
Results of the study are discussed.

33.   Eckenfels, E.J., et al. (1984).
Medical student counseling: The Rush Medical
College advisor program. Journal of Medical
Education, 59, 573-581.

This article describes the development of an
adviser program at Rush Medical College that
utilizes faculty members and provides
comprehensive counseling with continuity of
contact between adviser and student throughout
medical school. Evaluations used to determine
its efficiency are also discussed.

34.   Halgrin, R.P., & Halgrin, L.F. (1984).
An advising system for a large psychology
department. Teaching of Psychology, 11, 67-
70.

A serious problem for large psychology
departments is providing adequate advising for
its majors. Presented are successful attempts
to establish effective advising at the
University of Massachusetts, Amherst, in the
past and the current system, which is regarded
as the first successful advising system in the
past 15 years.

35.   Jaffe, W.F., & Huba, M.E. (1990).
Engineering students use of and satisfaction
with faculty and professional academic
advising systems. NACADA Journal, 10, 37-43.

A survey of 404 senior engineering students
investigated student use of advisers,
services, and information sought. Also
examined were patterns of use and satisfaction
related to student gender, grade point
average, and age. Higher-performing students
expressed more satisfaction, and younger
students used advisers more for some services.

36.   Krick, J.P., & Sobal, J. (1985). The
role of the faculty adviser in a family
medicine residency. Journal of Medical

Education, 60, 60-62.

A survey of medical college faculty advisers'
and residents' perceptions of the adviser's
role showed strong consensus. Students
desired less-regular meetings, more time for
advising, more written evaluations, more
informal nonacademic adviser participation,
and more group activities. A wide range of
expectations suggests a need for individual
negotiation.

37.   Lunneborg, P.W., & Baker, E.C. (1986).
Advising undergraduates in psychology:
Exploring the neglected dimension. Teaching
of Psychology, 13, 181-185.

This article presents a brief description and
evaluation of advising in departments of
psychology based on a 1985 national survey.
The survey notes, among other things, that the
"all faculty" model of advising was most
popular and that a majority of institutions
provided no advising rewards or system for
evaluation of advisers' performance.

38.   McCutcheon, W.R., et al. (1983).
Computer-assisted advising for dental
students. Journal of Dental Education, 47,
321-324.

Detailed descriptions are given of the five
computer-generated reports of the Student
Advising Information Package provided to
advisers for each advisee: 1) Family of
Patients; 2) Clinic Activity and Patient
Management; 3) Student Procedure Progress by
American Dental Association Code; 4)
Delinquent Appointments; and 5) Student-
Patient Appointment Summary.

39.   McGhee, M.B., & Cheek, J.G. (1990).
Assessment of the preparation and career
patterns of agricultural education graduates.

1975-1985. Journal of Agricultural Education, 31, 17-22.

In this article, responses from agricultural graduates determined their career patterns and assessed their perceptions of the effectiveness of selected aspects of the program. Agricultural casework, student teaching, and quality of faculty advising and teaching received high ratings.

40.   McMillian, M., & McKinney, K. (1985). Strategies for effective undergraduate advising in sociology. Resource material for teaching. Washington, D.C.: American Sociological Association, Teaching Resource Center. (ERIC Document Reproduction Service No. ED 273 209)

Many facets of advising sociology students are presented, including types of advisers, possible roles related to advising, and strategies for more effective advising. Specific techniques included are prototypes of paperwork, forms, and public relations materials. Also covered are academic, career, and personal counseling roles; curriculum-related roles; and teaching, internship and published roles. Many sample materials are appended.

41.   Milheim, W.D., Bredemeier, N.I., & Clemente, R. (1989). A computer-based, student-operated advising system for education majors. NACADA Journal, 9, 25-32.

A college of education computer-controlled advising system for undergraduate education majors is described. The computer program provided information in a variety of different areas including descriptions of various education programs, deadlines and applications, student teaching and other topics that may be helpful to the students.

Preliminary evaluation revealed that the
system was easy to use and effectively able to
answer the questions often asked by
undergraduate students in the college.

42.   Seeger, B.A., & McLean, D.D. (1985).
A comprehensive advising effort. NACADA
Journal, 5, 71-76.

A comprehensive advising system for physical
education and leisure study students is
described, including how it evolved, its
limitations, and what has been learned from
those limitations. The department developed a
computerized academic performance evaluation
system which developed competency areas for
evaluation of student growth and progress,
required periodic interviews at various levels
of academic development, and required periodic
contact between faculty adviser and student.
Each staff member would continue to perform
traditional advising functions in addition to
new functions. Most important in the whole
process was the increased role of the student
services coordinator.

43.   Wankat, P.C. (1986).   Current advising
practices and how to improve them.
Engineering Education, 76, 213-216.

This article reports on two surveys which
explored current advising and counseling
practices in chemical engineering departments.
The first consisted of a short questionnaire
sent to all chemical engineering departments
in the United States and Canada. The second
was a longer questionnaire sent to students
and counselors at two schools.

D. **Computer Assisted Advising**

44.   Abel, J. (1985). Using a computer data
base in an advising center. Journal of
College Student Personnel, 26, 166-167.

A computer data base was implemented to
identify the kind of advising contacts
advisers were having with freshmen who were
undecided as to a major. The data base
followed academic progress of these students
through their college experience.

45.   Appleby, D.C. (1989). The
microcomputer as an academic advising tool.
Teaching of Psychology, 16, 156-159.

Explains a microcomputer application that aids
the academic advising process. Results
indicate that this process makes students more
responsible for their future and has
beneficial effects on computer literacy,
student recruitment, career and graduate
school planning, early mentoring, and the
quality of letters of recommendations and
resumes.

46.   Bellenger, J.E., & Bellenger, D.N.
(1987). Guidelines for computerizing your
information system for academic program
counseling: Dealing with people problems.
NASPA Journal, 24, 53-60.

The value of computerized systems in freeing
counselors from excessive paperwork and
allowing them time to provide improved student
services is described. Also offered are
guidelines for designing and implementing an
effective information system for career and
academic counseling. Benefits, desirable
system characteristics, basic components of an
information system, behavioral problems to
anticipate, and steps to minimize
dysfunctional behavior are provided.

47.   Brewer, C.R., & Roller, J.M. (1985).
Orienting new students to computerized
registration: Providing opportunities for
academic advising. College and University,
60, 180-184.

A four-week summer preregistration program
provides students with opportunities for
individualized academic counseling while
registering via a computer. Suggestions for
handling computerized registration are given.
A fall follow-up is also described.

48.   Friedlander, J. (1983). Using the
computer to strengthen academic advisement
programs. Community College Review, 11, 52-
58.

This article suggests that many advisement
problems can be overcome through computer
usage, especially in performing time-consuming
clerical tasks. Also discussed are other uses
of the computer in the advising process, types
of information and services that can be
provided, and evaluation of a computer-
assisted advising program.

49.   Grupe, F.H., & Maples, M.F. (1992).
Preadmission student advising: A prototype
computerized system. NACADA Journal, 12, 42-
47.

Students who are clear about the match between
their needs and the institution's offerings
are more apt to enroll, schedule more wisely,
more likely to enjoy college, and are more apt
to persist to graduation. This article
describes a computer-assisted advising program
that was created originally to help high
school students select a major, but can also
be used by students who have had experience
with college-level course work. Although the
system is primarily an advice-giver and not an
instructional program, the student learns from
the questions that are asked to raise
consciousness about factors to consider when
selecting a major. The system is intended to
augment, not replace an academic adviser.

50.   Kramer, G.L., & Megerian, A. (1985).

Using computer technology to aid faculty advising. <u>NACADA</u> <u>Journal,</u> <u>5,</u> 51-61. The use of computer technology to assign preselected faculty advisers to students, enhancing faculty-student contact with incoming students is discussed. Also described is a computer program that creates an adviser file and links adviser information with students.

51. Kramer, G.L., & Peterson, E.D., & Spencer, R.W. (1984). Using computers in academic advising. In R. Winston, et al, (Eds.), <u>Developmental</u> <u>Advising.</u> San Francisco: Jossey-Bass.

This chapter discusses the uses of computer technology in academic advising. In addition to describing the landmark developments in computer-assisted advising, computer-assisted models are outlined. The analysis and design of computer files for a curriculum management system are critical elements of an effective program. Integrated information files updating requirements and tracking academic requirements are also important. Eight recommendations for any institution contemplating the development of expansion of a computer-assisted program are given.

52. Leigh, W., & Paz, N. (1991). Using visual programming to construct an information retrieval tool for student advising. <u>Microcomputers</u> <u>for</u> <u>Information</u> <u>Management,</u> <u>8,</u> 197-209.

The Course Advising Tool (CAT), a microcomputer-based information retrieval program that uses hypermedia and visual programming tools to help students develop their course schedules is described. The use of graphical cues and nonsequential navigation is discussed, and possible extensions to the system are also given.

53.   Potter, W. (1991). Freshman
registration by telephone: A low-tech model
for small colleges. College and University,
67, 31-35.

A telephone registration system for first year
students implemented at Alma College involves
having freshmen confer with advisers during
orientation week, then having the registrar's
office contact the advisers. Despite
limitations, the low-tech solution works well
at extremely low cost.

54.   Ray, H.N., Moore, W.K., & Oliver, J.E.
(1991). Evaluation of a computer-assisted
advising system. NACADA Journal, 11, 21-27.

This study examined the effectiveness of a
computer-assisted advising system that
replaced a more traditional faculty advising
system in a business school. Ninety-one
percent of the students sampled indicated the
computer system was as good or better than the
old manual system for providing advising
information. With the use of the computer-
printed advising form, about 40% of the
students indicated a need to see an adviser.
Another 40% did not. The evaluation survey
also showed that students differ considerably
with regard to the type and amount of advice
they want, and the amount of interaction they
desire with an adviser. The authors suggest
that a computer system designed for a
particular program, can meet the desires and
needs of students, faculty and the
institution.

55.   Spencer, R.W. (1991). "After" the
registration revolution. College and
University, 66, 209-212.

Touchtone telephone registration and related
computer student information system
technologies can provide more efficient use of

faculty, curriculum, and classroom space. Faculty, departments, and students all gain a degree of control. More in-depth and precise research must be undertaken and shared among institutions.

E. Peer Advising

56.   Barman, C.R., & Benson, P.A. (1981). Peer advising: A working model. NACADA Journal, 1, 33-40.

A peer advising program's components and evaluation are described and observations and conclusions drawn from a working model are provided. Use of peer advisers to assist in academic, personal, and career advising of new freshmen students has produced positive results and helped freshmen in their transition to the academic community. An adviser evaluation form is appended.

57.   Davis, B., & Ballard, M.R. (1985). Peer advisers: Agents of change for high-risk students. NACADA Journal, 5, 9-15.

Peer advisers can often help entering freshmen adjust to the environment of a large university by serving as experienced guides, advisers, confidantes, or friends, to whom the new students can easily relate. The article describes and discusses the program's effectiveness, especially with freshmen in academic difficulty. Results indicates that peer advising can increase retention and improve academic progress of high-risk students.

58.   Elliott, E.S. (1985). Academic advising with peer advisers and college freshmen. NACADA Journal, 5, 1-7.

An active and successful peer advising program in a college setting is discussed. The

assumption was that new students needed the
support and advice from an experienced
counselor to help them develop academic
competence, and upper-division students could
provide that support. The program was part of
a coordinated effort at the department,
college and university levels to promote
comprehensive academic advising models for use
with college students.

59.   Ender, S.C., & Winston, R.B. (Eds.)
(1984). Students as paraprofessional staff.
New Directions for Student Services, No. 27.
San Francisco: Jossey-Bass.

This volume examines how quality student
paraprofessional programs can have a positive
impact on the student client, the institution,
and the working paraprofessional. Quality
programs have written program goals; address
the normal developmental needs of college
students and paraprofessionals themselves;
have written job descriptions to guide the
working student paraprofessional; view
recruitment, selection and training as a
continuous, integrated process; practice
systematic supervision; and carry out sound
evaluation of staff and programs.

60.   Frisz, R.H. (1986). Peer counseling:
Establishing a network in training and
supervision. Journal of Counseling and
Development, 64, 457-459.

A peer counseling model is described and how
peer counselors can be used in other than
traditional counseling and advisement roles is
demonstrated. Peer counselors make it
possible for students to obtain help more
readily. Networking among peer counselors in
such areas as recruitment, training,
supervision, office administration, program
promotion, and development is discussed. Peer
counselors can be valuable to college

administration, but even more so to their fellow students.

61.   Frisz, R.H., & Lane, J.R. (1987). Student user evaluations of peer adviser services. Journal of College Student Personnel, 28, 241-245.

This article discusses the use of student user evaluations to determine the effectiveness of peer advising services. An evaluation instrument was given to each student who met with an assigned peer adviser. The questionnaire requested information about the advisee and evaluated the peer advising program. The results were very positive. Most students used the service for information related to college rules and major or career decision-making. Students felt more comfortable with peers and thought the program was an asset to the college.

62.   Habley, W.R. (1979). The advantages and disadvantages of using students as academic advisers. NASPA Journal, 17, 46-51.

The advantages and disadvantages of using undergraduate academic advisers are examined, including such advantages as program effectiveness, cost-containment, availability, accessibility, flexibility, and organizational input. Among the disadvantages are lack of continuity, accountability and objectivity. The author urges consideration of these disadvantages when recruiting, training and supervising the student advisers.

63.   Hartman, N.A., & Lagowski, J.M. (1982). Performance evaluation of peer advisors. Journal of College Student Personnel, 23, 78-79.

A detailed description of a formal evaluation process of peer advisers is given. The

evaluation is completed independently by the
peer adviser and his/her supervisor twice a
year. The completed evaluations are then
discussed at an appropriate time. The
evaluation form consists of a rating of
certain characteristics of the peer adviser,
additional comments related to job
performance, and the determination of specific
objectives to be met. It is stressed that
this formal evaluation is not to replace the
very important regular, ongoing evaluation.

64.   Hill, L. (1990). Facing life
transitions: A peer counseling program.
Journal of College Student Development, 31,
572-573.

This article discusses the Transition Peer
Counseling Program which provided support,
direction, and coping skills for students to
adapt to critical life transitions more
effectively. Peer counseling was offered in
three ways: a three-part peer counseled
series, dorm and classroom presentations, and
one-on-one peer counseling. A transition
training manual and student workbook were
written for the program. The Transition Peer
Counseling Program helped students more
effectively manage personal life changes.

65.   Holland, A., & Huba, M.E. (1989).
Psychosocial development among student
paraprofessionals in a college orientation
program. Journal of College Student
Personnel, 30, 100-105.

This study focused on the effect of
participation in an undergraduate service
project that was associated with the
orientation of new students. In this program,
selected undergraduates were trained as
paraprofessionals to present the university to
new students and their parents. The primary
purpose of the research was to determine if

participation positively influenced their
psychosocial development. Results indicated
that students who participated in a campus
service activity had significantly higher gain
scores that the control group on the
developmental variance of interdependent
tolerances. The results of this study suggest
that participation may also be an effective
means of stimulating certain developmental
characteristics in the participating students.

66.   Holly, K.A. (1987). Development of a
college peer counseling program. Journal of
College Student Personnel, 28, 285-286.

In this program the peer counselors were
available to all students for confidential
peer counseling on a daily basis. A problem
that the peer counseling program faced was
maintaining visibility and exposure to the
college community. Peer counselors indicated
that they used what they learned in their own
family situations and in their vocations.

67.   Locke, D.C., & Zimmerman, D.A. (1987).
Effects of peer counseling training on the
psychological maturity of black students.
Journal of College Student Personnel, 28, 525-
532.

In this study, the Defining Issues Test (DIT)
and the Sentence Completion Test (SCT) were
completed by black undergraduates who served
as peer mentors for one academic year. After
their mentoring experience, the experimental
group had higher ego development scores on the
SCT than at pretest, and their principal moral
reasoning scores on the DIT increased
slightly. It was concluded that the peer
counselor training program appeared to further
the psychological growth of this group of
black students in a predominantly white
university.

68.   Miller, K.L. (1989). Training peer
counselors to work on a multicultural campus.
Journal of College Student Development, 30,
561-562.

A peer counselor training program was
developed that capitalized on the cultural
diversity found within each training group.
Through cross-cultural discussions, supervised
experience, and explicit training, these
student peer counselors learned to recognize
the cultural obstacles underlying classroom
miscommunication. Additionally, these student
counselors augmented student personnel staff
in registration advising, alcohol and other
drug counseling, and other special services.
Peer counselor training was conducted as an
academic course.

69.   Puchkoff, S.C., & Fon-Padron, T.L.
(1990). Peer counseling: Implications for
personnel and vocational growth. Journal of
College Student Development, 31, 569-572.

This article reports on a study of students
who participated in a peer-counseling program
as undergraduate students. The study
attempted to determine the vocational
application of skills that graduates of an
undergraduate peer-counseling program
ascertained through their involvement and work
as peer counselors. Results of a survey
revealed that student participation as peer
counselors was assessed by respondents as one
of the most valuable growth experiences during
their college years.

70.   Russell, J.H., & Skinkle, R.R. (1990).
Evaluation of peer-adviser effectiveness.
Journal of College Student Development, 31,
388-394.

The results of a study examining the
effectiveness of a peer advising program is

reported as well as a study exploring the interaction between certain peer-helper characteristics and the effects on the students they help. The specific research questions were: 1) does a peer-advising orientation program influence first year students' levels of perceived membership within the university community?, 2) does peer-advising effectiveness influence participants' perceived membership in the university community?, and 3) are there particular personality characteristics found in highly effective peer-advisers and what is the interaction between these and participants' levels of perceived membership within the community? The results of this study suggest that the peer advising program had significant impact on the program's participants.

71.   Vohra, S., Rodolfa, E., De La Cruz, A., Vincent, C., & Bee-Gates, D. (1991). A cross-cultural format for peer counselors. Journal of College Student Development, 32, 82-84.

A training program that was successful in addressing cross-cultural issues with peer counselors is described. This workshop, with a slight change of original focus and format, has been used successfully with faculty and counselors, and as part of an orientation course. Feedback from students has been positive. Workshop participants not only learn about the concept of learning style characteristics, but also gained insight into their own learning style. Positive results were reported by both advisers and advisees.

72.   Winston, R.B., & Ender, S.C. (1988). Use of student paraprofessionals in divisions of college student affairs. Journal of Counseling and Development, 66, 466-473.

In this study, the chief student affairs
officers and the administrative heads of each
paraprofessional program at 118 higher
education institutions responded to a
questionnaire concerning the use of student
paraprofessionals. It was found that the most
extensive use of paraprofessionals was in
residence halls and orientation, and one third
of the institutions used student
paraprofessionals in student judiciaries,
student activities, counseling centers, career
planning and placement offices, and academic
advising. Further results are discussed.

73.   Zultowski, W.H., & Catron, D.W.
(1986). Students as curriculum advisers:
Reinterpreted. Journal of College Student
Personnel, 27, 199-204.

Student-advised freshmen were compared with
faculty-advised freshmen on their attitudes
toward advisers, academic progress variables,
and use of alternative campus referral
agencies. The data from the study suggest
that caution be exercised in using student
paraprofessional advisers. Advisees perceived
their student advisers as valuable sources of
information on academic matters. However,
student-advised undergraduates often had to
consult with other university offices for
further academic information. The authors
suggest that the student-advisers may be
providing their advisees with more subjective,
experiential advice than objective advice.

F. Residence Hall Advising

74.   Gershman, E.S., Anchors, S., &
Robbins, M.A. (1988). A multidisciplinary
faculty and peer advising program for
residentially based freshmen. Journal of
College Student Personnel, 29, 167-168.

The three primary goals established for a

residentially based advising program were the retention and satisfaction of the students, the efficiency of advising, and to create opportunities for faculty and student interaction outside the classroom. Objectives of the program were to make personal contact with all students soon after matriculation, to integrate academic affairs with student life, to clarify college and departmental policies, to help students plan academic programs, and to help undecided students explore options for majors by discussing their interests, abilities, and goals with student and faculty advisers from all disciplines in the college.

75.   Kuh, G.P., Schuh, J.H., & Thomas, R.O. (1985). Suggestions for encouraging faculty-student interaction in residence halls. NASPA, 22, 29-37.

Student-faculty interaction is a desired feature on most campuses, and the residence hall can be used as a vehicle for this interaction. In this program, faculty members are assigned to work with a group of residence hall students, eat at least one meal per week with the students, participate in their recreational and social activities, and engage in a limited amount of counseling and tutoring. The adoption of a program of this type entails careful consideration of elements related to faculty administration and residence life.

76.   Schein, H., Biggers, D., & Reese, V. (1986). The role of university residence halls in the academic advising process. NACADA Journal, 6, 67-75.

It is believed that residence halls are appropriate environments for developmentally oriented advising programs. This paper suggests ways for advising personnel to tap into this residence hall source. A

description of how residence halls are
structured is followed by an annotated access
scheme.   Included are models of how three Big-
Ten universities have incorporated advising
programs into their housing systems.

77.   Schein, H.K., & Bowers, P.M. (1992).
Using living/learning centers to provide
integrated campus services for freshmen.
Journal of the Freshman Year Experience, 4,
59-77.

This article presents an overview of living/
learning centers and a case study of an
evaluation of a living/learning center
academic program.   The structure of
living/learning centers is described including
facilities, credit classes, and guests-in-
residence programs.   The relationships between
academic and student affairs, and
administrative commitment and funding are
discussed.   The evaluation of the program at
the University of Illinois is described and it
confirmed the academic credibility of the
program and student satisfaction, in that 94%
of the students would choose the program
again.

Chapter 2

Developmental Advising

78.   Abel, J. (1988). Developmental advising through life roles: Leisure and leadership. <u>NACADA</u> <u>Journal,</u> <u>8,</u> 17-26.

Expanding developmental advising through life roles offers the opportunity for advising to realize its potential as a developmental and integrating force in higher education. The author suggests a model for moving into these life roles as well as ideas for academic advisers to use in incorporating leisure and leadership perspectives into their advising.

79.   Brown, T., & Rivas, M. (1993). Advising multicultural populations for achievement and success. In M.C. King (Ed.) <u>Academic</u> <u>advising:</u> <u>Organizing</u> <u>and</u> <u>delivering</u> <u>services</u> <u>for</u> <u>student</u> <u>success,</u> <u>New</u> <u>Directions</u> <u>for</u> <u>Community</u> <u>Colleges,</u> <u>No.</u> <u>82.</u> San Francisco: Jossey-Bass.

This chapter offers a developmental perspective on advising multicultural students. Effective advising of multicultural students requires an awareness and acknowledgment of cultural differences and a sensitivity to various individual biases. Possible interventions for students of color are provided.

80.   Carberry, J., Baker, M., Prescott, D.
(1986). Applying cognitive development theory
in the advising setting. NACADA Journal, 6,
13-18.

Knowledge of cognitive development theory can
enhance the "art of teaching" and an
understanding of student needs. The authors
translate cognitive theory concepts into useful
advising strategies. For advisers, the key is
to provide both support and challenge so as to
encourage a higher level of cognitive thinking.
Through careful recommendation of alternative
courses and structured activities, advisers can
facilitate a student's progress to higher
cognitive stages.

81. Chickering, A.W., & Reisser, L. (1993).
Education and identity (2nd ed.). San
Francisco: Jossey-Bass.

This revised version of Chickering's 1969
classic book updates his human development
framework that includes seven tasks that
college students must accomplish as they move
into adulthood. It includes new findings from
the last twenty-five years in such areas as
gender and multicultural differences and
describes policies and practices in higher
education that are designed to enrich
educational environments. Suggestions for
fostering student growth are also included.

82.   Crookston, B.B. (1972). A developmental
view of academic advising as teaching. Journal
of College Student Personnel, 13, 12-17.

The difference between developmental and
prescriptive advising is described in this
classic article. Developmental advising is
seen as the nature and quality of the
relationship between adviser and advisee.
Advising is viewed as a teaching function where
responsibilities are negotiated between student

and adviser.   In the developmental
relationship, both parties engage in a series
of developmental tasks, both learn, and
together they work out an agreement as to who
will take initiative and responsibility and who
will supply knowledge and skills.
Developmental advising also differs from
prescriptive advising in its view of abilities,
motivation, rewards, maturity, control,
learning output, and evaluation.

83.   Dickson, G.L. (1991).   Developmental
theory and organizational structure: An
integration.   NASPA Journal, 11, 202-215.

The author proposes an organizational structure
that integrates campuswide resources and
"focuses them on .... a human development
mission." The linking of organizational
structure and developmental goals is difficult
and rarely accomplished. To reach student
development goals, the author contends, student
development theory must be woven into an
institution's organizational structure. A
selected group of student affairs professionals
was ask to rate the potential contributions of
12 student services to each of Chickering's
developmental vectors. Academic advising,
residential life, and student activities were
rated as having the highest potential for
accomplishing these student developmental
tasks. A structural intervention model is
described which can link campus resources
together to provide a student development
approach.

84.   Ender, S.C., Winston, R.B., & Miller,
T.K. (1982). Academic advising as student
development.   In R.B. Winston, S.C. Ender, and
T.K. Miller (Eds.) Developmental approaches to
academic advising. New Directions for Student
Services, No. 17. San Francisco: Jossey-Bass.

If the idea of the whole person is to be

realized in American higher education,
principles of student development must be
formally integrated into the institution's
mission, goals, and program thrusts. Academic
advising is viewed as one existing vehicle that
can readily be refitted for this purpose. In
order for colleges to have a beneficial impact
on the intellectual and personality development
of students, academic and student affairs
divisions must work collaboratively. Academic
advising should be the touchstone for the
integrated efforts.

85.   Gordon, V.N. (1992). History and roots
of academic advising. In Handbook of academic
advising. (pp. 4-17). Westport, CT: Greenwood
Press.

This chapter traces the history of
developmental academic advising in higher
education and provides developmental
definitions of the advising process. It
presents theoretical frameworks on which
advising is based including student, adult,
career, moral, and learning theories. The
author contends that developmental theory can
enhance understanding of students as they
engage in the academic advising process.

86.   Gordon, V.N. (1988). Developmental
advising. In W.R. Habley (Ed.) The status and
future of academic advising (pp. 104-115).
Iowa City: American College Testing Program.

Developmental advising is defined in this
chapter, and theoretical underpinnings are
described. Summary of developmental theory is
outlined and the use of theory in practical
situations is provided. Developmental advising
goals, strategies, and techniques are detailed
for individual as well as programmatic
advising.

87. Kramer, G.L., Taylor, L., Chynoweth, B., &

Jensen, J. (1987). Developmental academic advising: A taxonomy of services. NASPA Journal, 24, 27-31.

This article reviews research on key student academic needs and presents them in a taxonomic model on how to focus on student development in academic advising. It also addresses the different needs of each academic class and discusses potential delays to student progress through ineffective advising. Coordination of institutional resources to promote student development is discussed.

88.   Miller, T.K., & McCaffrey, S.S. (1982). Student development theory: Foundations for academic advising. In R.B. Winston, S.C. Ender, and T.K. Miller (Eds.) Developmental approaches to academic advising. New Directions for Student Services, No. 17. San Francisco: Jossey-Bass.

Student development theories, specifically psychosocial development and intellectual development, provide a framework for understanding students and for guiding the structure and interaction of the academic advising process. Effective advising programs can be founded on theories of human development, which can guide advisers as they seek to create environments conducive to students' educational and personal growth.

89.   Perry, W.G. (1970). Forms of intellectual and ethical development in the college years. New York: Holt, Rinehart and Winston.

This book outlines the cognitive development theory of William Perry. The theory was derived from interviewing students at Harvard University over an extensive period. Students were encouraged to think and talk about topics of importance to them. From these protocols

Perry derived his theory of how students change
and grow during the college years. This volume
outlines the nine positions of development in
Perry's scheme. It also describes three
alternatives to growth: temporizing, retreat
and escape. Implications of the study for
practical purposes are also given.

90.   Raushi, T.M. (1993). Developmental
academic advising. In M.C. King (Ed.),
Academic advising: Organizing and delivering
services for student success, New Directions
for Community Colleges (pp. 5-19). San
Francisco: Jossey-Bass.

Developmental advising is defined. Key
developmental theories are reviewed and their
applications for advising in two-year colleges
are discussed.

91.   Winston, R.B. (1990). The Student
Development Task and Lifestyle Inventory: An
approach to measuring students' psychosocial
development. Journal of College Student
Development, 31, 108-120.

An instrument titled the Student Development
Task and Lifestyle Inventory designed to
measure certain aspects of Chickering's theory
of the psychosocial development of traditional
age college students was developed. The
process used in constructing the instrument is
described, and reliability and validity studies
are summarized. Studies conducted with
different student subpopulations at several
institutions showed acceptable reliability
estimates for the SDTLI. Correctional studies
were also conducted with related well-
established instruments.

92.   Winston, R., Miller, T., Ender, S., &
Grites, T. (1984). Developmental academic
advising. San Francisco: Jossey-Bass.
This volume is composed of chapters written by

many advising professionals on topics related
to advising from a developmental perspective.
Part One: academic advising for student
development, provides a theoretical foundation
and a description of current practices. The
advising process is described in Part Two which
includes strategies such as educational and
career planning and advising students with
special needs. Part Three describes delivery
systems and the institutional context,
administrative issues, legal issues and
training. The last part describes model
advising programs.

93.   Winston, R.B., Ender, S.C., & Miller,
T.K. (Eds.) (1982). Developmental approaches to
academic advising. New Directions for Student
Services, No. 17. San Francisco: Jossey-Bass.

The academic advising process presents the
opportunity to extend student developmental
concepts beyond the realm of traditional
cocurricular programming into the whole
institution. It can also institutionalize an
integrated approach to educating students that
addresses personal as well as intellectual
development. This sourcebook transfers student
development theory to those who deal directly
with students through the advising process.

Chapter 3

Special Populations

A. Adult Students

94.   Bitterman, J.E. (1985). Academic
advising and adult education: An emerging
synthesis. NACADA Journal, 5, 29-33.

Academic advising programs will grow
increasingly important in the future with the
proliferation of adult students in higher
education, because the presence of older
students will focus more attention on innately
developmental issues such as the stimulation
of lifelong learning, career planning, and
adjustment to college life. Faculty members
must become more aware of the special needs
and skills of adult students. Faculty members
should be invited to workshops on adult
students, and those who have shown
effectiveness in advising adult students
should be recognized.

95.   Brenden, M.A. (1986). Pioneering new
support systems for non-traditional
baccalaureate students: Interactional
advising and peer mentoring. NACADA Journal,
6, 77-82.

While students of traditional college age once

dominated the undergraduate ranks to the near
exclusion of older students, non-traditional-
aged students now constitute a significant
proportion of that population. Interactional
advising and peer monitoring are valuable
supplements to the traditional faculty-student
advising relationship.

96.   Champagne, D.E., & Petitpas, A.
(1989). Planning developmental interventions
for adult students. NASPA Journal, 26, 265-
271.

While the developmental tasks of traditional-
aged college students and adult learners may
differ, the transition process may hold
similarities. Quite often, however, student
affairs interventions have been targeted for
the specific developmental tasks of the
traditional student. This article suggests
that student affairs professionals need to
give greater consideration to the
developmental needs of adult learners. In
particular, it proposes a framework for
planning developmental interventions for them.

97.   Dannells, M., Rivera, N.L., & Knall-
Clark, J.E. (1992). Potentials to meet and
promises to keep: Empowering women through
academic and career counseling. College
Student Journal, 26, 237-242.

One of the fastest growing student groups is
reentry women. Although women have the
ability to study any discipline, they are
often discouraged by differential treatment in
the curriculum and by the nature of the
administrative and faculty structures of our
educational system. This article identifies
areas where advisers and counselors can assist
nontraditional women to recognize their
potential and realize maximum benefits from
college. Counselors are sometimes guilty of
perpetuating occupational segregation

because of their personal sex-biased belief
systems. In addition to academic and career
advising, the reentry women often needs
counseling for self-esteem and changing family
relationships while in school. Stress
management and values clarification are ways
of helping women students deal with their
expectations and disappointments. Services
and programs to assist nontraditional women
are described to help them through the
transitions they are experiencing.

98.   Dean, G.J., Eriksen, J.P., &
Lindamood, S.A. (1987). Adults in mid-career
change: Case studies for advisors. NACADA
Journal, 7, 16-26.

Academic advisors must be able to understand
the needs and motivations of adult learners
and to develop advising skills and programs in
response to these needs. The purpose of this
paper is to outline some of the motivations
and needs of both full-time and part-time
adult learners who are in transition from work
to school and to offer suggestions to academic
advisors on how to meet those needs.

99.   DeSilvestro, F.R. (Ed.) (1981).
Advising and counseling adult learners. New
Directions for Continuing Education, No. 10.
San Francisco: Jossey-Bass.

This sourcebook is a resource for
practitioners who would like to establish or
revise counseling programs for adult learners.
It also provides ideas for improving
counseling skills in dealing with adult
learners, and suggests topics for research
concerning the types of skills needed by those
who counsel adult learners and those who teach
counselors of adult learners.

100.   Mounty, L.H. (1991). Involving
nontraditional students in the career planning

process at an urban institution. Journal of
Higher Education Management, 6, 43-48.

Nontraditional students, especially adults,
are encouraged to participate in the career
planning process. Existing programs, new
scheduling services and new programming have
been organized to coordinate the services in
the following areas: freshman orientation,
academic advising, student activities, and the
career center.

101.   Polson, C.J., & Eriksen, J.P. (1988).
The impact of administrative support and
institutional type on adult learner services.
NACADA Journal, 8, 7-16.

This study described and examined the scope of
existing services for adult learners enrolled
in higher education. Two analyses were
performed, one to review the effect of
institutional type on services provided and
the second to understand the impact of
perceived administrative support on efforts to
serve this student population. The
implications of the findings for academic
advisers are addressed.

102.   Rossman, M.H., & Rossman, M.E. (Eds.)
(1990). Applying adult development
strategies. San Francisco: Jossey-Bass.

Adult educators must not only be aware of how
adults develop throughout their postadolescent
lifetimes, but also be able to translate this
awareness into practical action. The goal of
this volume is to present an overview of adult
development as well as examples of strategies
to put this knowledge into action.

103.   Terrell, P.S. (1990). Adapting
institutions of higher education to serve
adult students' needs. NASPA Journal, 27,
241-247.

This article explores the developmental needs
of adult students from age and gender
perspectives. Implications for adapting
academic and student services to this
population are explored. Recommendations for
adapting these services to accomodate the
special needs of adult students are given.

104.   Wilkie, C.J., & Thompson, C.A.
(1993). First-year reentry women's
perceptions of their classroom experiences.
Journal of the Freshman Year Experience, 5,
69-90.

This research project shows that first-year
reentry women perceive the affectional aspects
of their classroom experiences much more
negatively than other first-year students.
They report feeling significantly more
alienated, self-conscious, "stupid,"
voiceless, fearful, and inadequate than their
first-year peers. There is a major shift in
these negative perceptions that was found to
occur between the first and second years.
Recommendations are presented for instructors
and the higher education system.

B. Student Athletes

105.   Benson, M.T. (Ed.) (1991). A
statistical analysis of the predictions of
graduation rates for college student
athletics. NCAA academic performance study
(Report 91-02). Overland Park, KS: National
Collegiate Athletic Association. (ERIC
Document Reproduction Service No. ED 335 991)

Data for 82 schools and 4,845 student athletes
are analyzed based on 5-year graduation
results for 1984 and 1985. Data provided
includes patterns of college outcomes,
including graduation rates for white, black,
male, and female student athletes; a summary
of descriptive statistics; predictive

graduation rates; moderator variables; and the
accuracy and fit improvement of high school
grade point average and standardized test
score variables broken down into separate
demographic groups. Differences between the
average student at the school and the student
athlete are also provided. A chronological
summary of academic persistence prediction for
1984 and 1985 student athletes is given.

106.   Bland, F.W. (1985). Intercollegiate
athletic competition and students' educational
and career plans. <u>Journal</u> <u>of</u> <u>College</u> <u>Student</u>
<u>Personnel,</u> <u>26,</u> 115-118.

This study compared the self-reports of
educational and career plans of upperclass and
lower class students within two NCAA Division
I colleges and two NCAA Division III colleges.
Freshmen and sophomore male athletes at both
colleges did not formulate mature educational
and career plans compared to male non-
athletes. Upperclass athletes, however,
formulated mature plans nearly as well as non-
athletes. Possible explanations are that
older athletes are more realistic about the
future, or that those younger athletes who are
not attentive to their educational plans may
drop or be dropped from school.

107.   Chartrand, J.M., & Lent, R.W. (1987).
Sports counseling: Enhancing the development
of the student-athlete. <u>Journal</u> <u>of</u> <u>Counseling</u>
<u>and</u> <u>Development,</u> <u>66,</u> 164-167.

The academic and personal development of
intercollegiate athletes is a growing concern
among academic administrators and student
affairs professionals. The authors explore
two problems, role conflict and athletic
retirement, commonly faced by student-
athletes. Also, they describe several
potentially useful intervention models based
on a psychoeducational approach and suggest

some directions for future research in aiding
understanding of student-athlete development.

108.   Edwards, H. (1991). Democratic
pluralism: Placing African-American student-
athletes in the context of a new agenda for
higher education. NACADA Journal, 11, 28-108.

The author contends that African American
student-athletes' patterned negative outcomes
can be reliably understood and effectively
addressed only if due consideration is given
to social, cultural, and political forces that
seriously impact but that emanate far beyond
the institutional functioning of academia and
sport. Democratic pluralism is posed as an
alternative to both established Black liberal
and incipient Black neoconservatism change
regimens, as well as other strategems relative
to advancement in sport, education, and
society.

109.   Ender, S.C. (1983). Assisting high
academic risk athletes: Recommendations for
the academic adviser. NACADA Journal, 3, 1-
10.

An advising program for high-risk athletes
using a student development approach is
described. Athletes' views on the people and
events in their environment affecting academic
performance and recommendations for their
advisers are also outlined.

110.   Gibson, D.E., & Creamer, D.G.
(1987). Perceptions of academic support by
student athletes. College Student Affairs
Journal, 7, 43-49.

At six institutions, student athletes were
given a semi-structured interview on their
career goals and their sources of academic
support. The responses indicated that
athletes were influenced more by people than

programs. Coaches and academic advisers strongly influenced the students' use of academic support services. Student attitudes toward study and support systems developed after enrollment and were related to the amount and consistency of academic encouragement given by college personnel.

111.   Gordon, R.L. (1986). Issues in advising student athletes. NACADA Journal, 6, 81-86.

Four issues involving the student athlete are identified as important to academic advising: the relationship between athletic participation and academic performance, individual differences among student athletes, the possible conflict in the roles of student and athlete, and the debate over the need for special programs for student athletes.

112.   Gurney, G.S., Robinson, D.C., & Fyetakis, L.M. (1983). Athletic academic counseling with NCAA Division I institutions: A national profile of staffing, training and service. Athletic Administration, 17, 9-13.

This study investigated trends of staffing and academic support services among athletically competitive institutions. Results suggest steady growth in the staffing of counseling professionals and programming emphasizing learning skill development. The results also indicate that programs still lack many academic support and psychological services for this student population.

113.   Gurney, G.S., & Johnson, S.P. (1986). Advising the student-athlete. NACADA Journal, 6, 27-29

This article reviews institutional studies describing the academic preparation and subsequent performance of student-athletes and discusses their implication for academic advising. Academic advisers are viewed as vital to the orientation process and the authors suggest that freshmen avoid a course considered high risk so a positive start might be provided. Advisers and support services are discussed and the advising process can create a necessary climate of encouragement and support. Advisers are agents for the institution for determining its level of commitment to the student-athlete.

114.   Henderson, G. (1986).   Advising Black student-athletes.   NACADA Journal, 6, 3-11.

One reason a disproportionate number of ethnic minority group athletes in general and Black athletes in particular do not excel in academics, may be attributed to inadequate advising. The helping relationship, what Black student-athletes need, and who can do the job are discussed in this article.

115.   Jordan, J.M., & Denson, E.L. (1990). Student services for athletes: A model for enhancing the student-athlete experience. Journal of Counseling & Development, 69, 95-97.

This article describes a comprehensive program designed to attend to the developmental needs of student-athletes. Academic monitoring is discussed as different from academic advising. During the monitoring process both students and faculty are involved. Also discussed are consulting and outreach services. Personal counseling services are described. The program's location outside the athletic department is seen as a positive feature. A broader, university-wide perspective as well as unlimited access to many student development resources is possible because of this location.

116.   Kramer, H.C. (1986). Faculty
advising: Help for student-athletes? NACADA
Journal, 6, 67-79.

Advising of student-athletes is discussed as
an institutional rather than an individual or
educational endeavor. A general system
framework for thinking about the issue is
provided to initiate a dialogue about the
understanding of and developmental change in
advising student-athletes.

117.   Lanning, W. (1982). The privileged
few: Special counseling needs of athletes.
Journal of Sport Psychology, 4, 19-23.

The author indicates that many academic
counselors are not trained to deal with the
special needs of student athletes. Self-image
is difficult for athletes who come from high
schools where they were stars, to college
where the competition is much tougher. Many
students aspire to play professional sports
although very few do. Career development is
important for student athletes who will soon
complete their eligibility. Injuries can also
force athletes to make adjustments. Training
counselors appropriately and educating coaches
is the key to dealing more effectively with
the special needs of the student athlete.

118.   Roper, L.D., & McKenzie, A. (1988).
Academic advising: A developmental model for
black student-athletes. NASPA Journal, 26,
91-98.

A model for a comprehensive developmental
approach to advising Black college athletes is
presented. The model consists of five
dimensions: symbolization, alocentrism,
integration, stability, and autonomy. When
all these developmental, interdependent
dimensions are balanced, the student-athlete
can grow in a well-rounded way.

119.   Schubert, A.F., & Schubert, G.W.
(1986). The student-athlete: Ethical and
legal issues. NACADA Journal, 6, 53-66.

Recruiters evaluate the student athlete in
three major categories: athletic potential,
academic potential, and personal character.
The student athlete and families of the
student athlete should also evaluate the
institution. The institution could be
evaluated in such areas as appropriate
academic offerings, special assistance
available to students, emphasis of the
institution upon graduate or undergraduate
preparation, graduation rate of athletes, and
placement of graduates.

120.   Sowa, C.J., & Gressard, C.F. (1983).
Athletic participation: Its relationship to
student development. Journal of College
Student Personnel, 24, 236-239.

This study sought to determine if differences
between athletes and non-athletes exist on the
achievement of developmental tasks.
as defined by Chickering. There were no
differences in overall achievement of athletes
when compared to non-athletes, but further
analysis suggested that there may be some
individual developmental tasks on which
athletes have more difficulty, such as
developing mature relationships with peers.
The authors caution, however, that this may be
the result of how this variable is defined
since participation in some sports does not
always encourage greater independence and
individuality. The authors suggest that
academic and personal counseling should be
included and programs provide a systematic
method of evaluating the developmental stages
of the student.

121.   Underwood, C., Jr. (1986). Advising
of black student-athletes: Twelve

recommendations. NACADA Journal, 6, 19-21.

Because of their social, educational and
economic status, black student-athletes bring
concerns to their institutions that need
addressing. Twelve recommendations are
provided that could be an excellent foundation
for helping black athletes achieve their full
academic potential.

122.   Zingg, P.J. (1982). Advising the
student athlete. Educational Record, 63, 16-
19.

The author makes a case for treating the
student athlete with the same justice,
compassion, and sensitivity that should
characterize an institution's relationship
with all students. Honest, responsible
admissions counseling is critical, and follow-
up advising should focus on developing a
collegiate perspective.

C. **Commuter Students**

123.   Elder, P., & Wilson, P.A. (Eds.)
(1986). Commuters. (Special Issue). NASPA
Journal, 24, (1).

This special issue focuses on commuter
students who are defined as those who do not
live in campus housing, fraternity or sorority
housing, or off-campus housing in an area
immediately surrounding the campus. Four
articles describe prerequisites for serving
commuter students, including a profile of the
characteristics and demographics of commuter
students, developing a sensitivity to the
commuter perspective, designing the campus
environment for commuter students, and
developing a sense of belonging in commuter
students. Other articles suggest how small
institutions can develop successful programs
for commuter students, and how Greek systems

can operate positively on a commuter campus.
Sources of information are given, including
journals and organizations for student affairs
personnel working with commuter students.
National standards for establishing and
maintaining a commuter program are given.

124.   Sloan, P., & Wilmes, M.B. (1989).
Advising from the commuter perspective.
NACADA Journal, 9, 67-75.

This article redefines adult learners as part
of the broader commuter student population and
identifies four areas of concern common to
student who commute: mobility, integrating
support systems, multiple life roles, and
involvement in campus life. Implications of
these concerns in the advising setting are
discussed, and four roles for advisers working
with adult commuters are addressed: a)
dealing with issues of transition, b)
translating the institution to the student, c)
assisting the student in forming campus
connections, and d) advocating on behalf of
the student.

125.   Stewart, S.S. (Ed.) (1983). Commuter
students: Enhancing their educational
experiences. New Directions for Student
Services, No. 24. San Francisco: Jossey-
Bass. This monograph is designed to assist
educators in changing the campus environment
in order to enhance the learning opportunities
of commuter students. Different chapters
define commuter students, show how
institutions can conduct self-studies of their
responses to commuter students, show how the
development of commuter students can be
enhanced by parental involvement, and describe
how developmental concepts can be applied to
the design of programs for commuter students.
Organizations involved in commuter affairs are
listed in the final chapter, which includes a
bibliography and a subject index.

D. Disabled Students

126.   Bogart, S.K., Eidelman, L.J., &
Kujawa, C.L. (1988). Helping learning
disabled students in college. Education
Digest, 53, 48-51.

This article makes the following points and
recommendations about learning disabled
students. 1) learning disabled college
students are capable of mastering academic
content; 2) alternative methods for learning
and/or demonstrating this mastery may be
needed; 3) instructors, counselors, and
administrators must be sensitive to the
personal/social and self-esteem issues
affecting learning disabled students; 4)
support and resources must be available to the
students without stigmatizing them; and 5)
support and resources must be available to
faculty and administrators as they learn how
to deal effectively with learning disabled
students.

127.   Farrell, M.L., & Harckham, L.D.
(1988). Attitude of college personnel toward
learning disabled college students. Journal
of Postsecondary Education and Disability, 6,
7-13.

A questionnaire designed to assess attitudes
toward learning disabled student was completed
by faculty members and student services staff
members who were attending workshops on
working with learning disabled students. A t-
test comparison revealed that the student
services staff members scored higher than the
faculty members, which indicated that they had
a more favorable attitude toward learning
disabled students.

128.   Frank, K., & Wade, P. (1993).
Disabled services in postsecondary education:
Who's responsible for what? Journal of

College Student Development, 34, 26-30.

Federal legislation has mandated that
postsecondary institutions make special
accommodations and adjustments to insure that
students are not discriminated upon based on a
disability. Responsible institutional
decision making needs to be based on key legal
requirements for providing accommodations to
disabled students. This article discusses the
identification of the disabling condition, how
to define the "qualified handicapped student,"
how discrimination is addressed under the law,
and when accommodations need to be and when
they don't need to be provided. It is
imperative that all campus agencies, such as
student affairs and advising offices have a
clear working knowledge of these requirements
so prospective students are not provided with
inaccurate information, enrolled students are
advised properly, and university presidents
have access to clear information on which to
base decisions.

129.   Kramer, K. (1988). Computer
accessibility for students with disabilities.
Academic Computing, 3, 26.

The academic computing needs of students with
disabilities must be ascertained and the
appropriate adaptive technology selected to
serve them. Adaptive technology allows
students with disabilities to gain access to
computers through current modifications at the
hardware, software, and firmware levels.
Software packages, for example, have been
developed to assist with test proctoring,
learning-style assessments, cognitive-skills
training, vocational evaluation and career
guidance, and job placement assistance.

E. Graduate and Professional Students

130.   Barger, R.R., & Mayo-Chamberlain, J.

(1983). Advisor and advisee issues in doctoral education. Journal of Higher Education, 54, 407-432.

This article reviews the developmental issues associated with advisor-advisee relationships in graduate education with a major focus on the creation of developmental settings for advisees. Advisor and advisee perspectives are interrelated and this relationship is discussed. Consideration is given to the academic, professional, and community settings that influence their relationship.

131.   Brown, R.D., & Krager, L. (1985). Ethical issues in graduate education: Faculty and student responsibilities. Journal of Higher Education, 56, 403-418.

A framework for examining the ethical responsibilities of faculty and students in graduate school is presented and illustrated. Based on five principles (autonomy, nonmaleficence, beneficence, justice, and fidelity), this framework is intended to encourage discussion of the mutual responsibilities of graduate education and professional development.

132.   Kammerer, D. (1986). Advisors' perceptions of their advising experiences with their doctoral students during the dissertation. Unpublished doctoral dissertation, The Ohio State University, Columbus, Ohio.

The expressed perceptions of experienced, male advisors were obtained during in-depth, tape recorded interviews. Three major implications for practice were reported in this study: 1) although advisors perceived the dissertation experience of their students to be creative, they offered few suggestions or examples of efforts they initiated or entertained to provide for more creative dissertation activity of their students, 2) advisors reported that the demands of the advisor-student relationship as it relates to the advising time, interest in the topic, and quality of work, often resulted in greater time demand on the advisor, which was often perceived as difficult or troublesome, and 3) the quality of the advisor and student interpersonal relationship related directly to the quality of the dissertation advising experience.

133.   Kirk, J., & Wysocki, J. (1991). Factors influencing choice of graduate program and some implications for student advisement. NACADA Journal, 11, 14-20.

The purpose of this study was to investigate the career and educational motivations of graduate students in selected programs. A questionnaire was developed from 11 factors found in the literature which influence student choices of majors and programs. Two-letter Holland codes and other information about students' personal and occupational backgrounds were collected. The results suggest that students select their graduate programs mainly on the basis of two factors: opportunity and quality. Many suggestions for how the results have implications for advising are given.

134.   Vickio, C.J., & Tack, M.W. (1989). Orientation programming for graduate students: An institutional imperative. NACADA Journal, 9, 37-42.

An extensive orientation program for new graduate students is described. Its purpose is to introduce enrolling students to their new academic and institutional roles, the faculty and administrative personnel, and help ease their fears and misconceptions regarding

their assimilation into their graduate
department. University services and support
programs as well as local community resources
are introduced. Also covered are graduate
responsibilities such as research and teaching
assistantships. Other aspects of the
orientation program are included.

F. High-Ability Students

135.   Friedman, P.G., & Jenkins-Friedman,
R.C. (1986). Fostering academic excellence
through honors programs. New Directions for
Teaching and Learning, No 25. San Francisco:
Jossey Bass.

The goal of this volume is to enlarge readers'
awareness of various operating principles and
options for honors education by addressing the
unique needs and characteristics of honor
students. Two sources were incorporated in
this collection. The first was to draw on the
experiences of individuals with many years
experience working in the honors field; the
second consists of people practicing and
studying honors teaching at precollege levels.
The first two thirds of this volume are
concerned with issues involved in
administering a centralized honors education.
These include a portrait of contemporary
honors education; the controversies inherent
in an honors education; principles for honors
selection; minority and gender issues; honors
advising within and outside the classroom; and
community colleges and honors programs. The
remaining chapters deal directly with
specifics of teaching honors students. They
cover the design and supervision of honors
programs, group dynamics, and finally,
recommendations for fostering excellence in
higher education.

136.   Gordon, V.N. (1983). Meeting the
career development needs of undecided honors

students. Journal of College Student
Development, 24, 82-83.

Undecided honors freshmen were compared to
regular undecided freshmen to determine if
their approaches to academic and career
decisions were different. Although interest
patterns were not significantly different,
honors students were less decided about a
major and had higher anxiety scores.
Undecided honors students need special adviser
attention since they are multipotential, feel
more pressure to choose, may narrow their
choice prematurely, and may need more time to
find their occupational identity. Suggestions
for incorporating knowledge of these
characteristics into advising programs are
offered.

137.   Gordon, V.N. (1992). Advising
special populations: High-ability students.
In V.N. Gordon, Handbook of academic
advising, (pp. 98-101). Westport, CT:
Greenwood Press.

This entry describes the characteristics of
high-ability students including performance,
motivation, and career issues. Concurrent
enrollment of high school students is
discussed. Honors programs and other
opportunities in both two-year and four-year
colleges are briefly outlined. Faculty
attitude and behavior in regard to advising
students vary greatly. Several advising
suggestions are made.

138.   Kerr, B.A., & Colangelo, N. (1988).
The college plans of academically talented
students. Journal of Counseling and
Development, 67, 42-48.

This study indicated that academically
talented students as a group are somewhat
narrow in their academic major choices but

broad in their extracurricular interests.
They were uninterested in personal counseling
but demanding of career help, independent
study, and honors opportunities. This study
also showed quantitative rather than
qualitative differences between two levels of
talent, those highly talented or "high
average" as determined by ACT percentiles.
Patterns of academic major choices,
extracurricular interests, and desire for
academic services were similar for two groups,
but highly talented students showed more
extreme results.

139.   Lovely, R. (1987, February).
Selection of undergraduate majors by high
ability students: Sex differences and the
attrition of science majors. (ASHE 1987
Annual Meeting Paper). Paper presented at the
Annual Meeting of the Association for the
Study of Higher Education, San Diego, CA.
(ERIC Document Reproduction Service No. ED 281
451)

The relative participation of high ability
male and female college students as natural
science majors and attrition of these students
from the sciences to other majors were studied
at a highly selective, comprehensive research
university. The effects of math aptitude and
precollege science achievement on selection of
the major were assessed. Gender differences
in precollege intentions to major in a natural
science appear to be largely based on relative
differences in high school science
preparation. Well-prepared females were as
likely to intend to major in the natural
sciences as comparable men, but females had
lower overall levels of preparation.
Attrition of science majors appears similar
for the best prepared men and women. Less-
well-prepared women, however, were more likely
to abandon natural science majors than
comparable men.

G. Transfer Students

140.   Ford, J. (1986). Promoting advising
and course articulation between a university
and community colleges. NACADA Journal, 6,
93-98.

The steps involved in developing course
articulation tables between a university and
community colleges is described. Some
objectives for implementing this procedure
were to educate the faculty regarding
appropriate courses to be substituted for
general studies required courses, building
rapport with the community colleges, and
fostering academic advising by providing
adequate materials and support services.

141.   Hogan, R.R. (1986). An update on
reverse transfers to two-year colleges.
Community/Junior College Quarterly of Research
and Practice, 10, 295-306.

This study examined the ways in which newly
enrolled reverse transfer students, defined as
students who transfer from four-year colleges
to two-year institutions, differ from newly
enrolled native two-year college students.
The official student records at 13 two-year
colleges were examined. Analysis of variance
revealed that, compared to the native
students, the reverse transfer students were
more likely to be older, married, employed,
and enrolled part-time. In addition, the
reverse transfer students earned higher grades
than did the new native students and were more
likely to be planning to earn credits toward a
four-year degree, or in the event they already
had a degree, to be taking classes for
personal enrichment.

142.   Newhouse, J.S., & McNamara, A.
(1982). The transfer student: A dual
approach. NACADA Journal, 2, 24-29.

Community college students need help with
problems of credit evaluation, articulation,
course placement, evaluation of work
experience, and academic advising. This
article describes a program that includes
college fairs, campus visits, and publication
of a transfer guide series.

H. Undecided Students and Major-Changers

143.   Anderson, B.C., Creamer, D.G., &
Cross, L.H. (1989). Undecided, multiple
change, and decided students: How different
are they? NACADA Journal, 9, 46-50.

The purpose of this study was to provide a
descriptive profile of the undecided student
and compare these students with decided and
multiple change students. Results indicate
that undecided students are no different from
other students and the condition or state of
undecidedness about major upon initial
enrollment does not signal "problems ahead"
for these students.

144.   Buescher, K.L., Johnston, J.A.,
Lucas, E.B., & Hughey, K.F. (1989). Early
intervention with undecided college students.
Journal of College Student Development, 30,
375-376.

This study sought to determine if an early
intervention that exposed students to
occupational information, assistance with
organization and awareness about self and
occupations, and support, reinforcement and
encouragement, would have an effect on the
vocational identity of entering college
freshmen. The results indicated that students
who received early intervention were able to
develop a clearer and more stable picture of
their goals, interests, and skills.

145.   Elliott, E.S. (1984). Change of

major and academic success.   NACADA Journal,
4, 39-45.

This study explores the effects that scores on
a career-maturity scale and college experience
have on the change of major status of four
groups of college students who: declared
their major during their freshman year,
changed their major once, changed their major
two or more times, and entered the university
as provisional or advanced outstanding
students. The results revealed no significant
difference, on academic success, between those
who declared majors, changed once, changed
more than once, and those who changed from a
provisional or advanced standing.

146.   Gordon, V.N., & Steele, G.E. (1992).
Advising major-changers: Students in
transition.   NACADA Journal, 12, 22-27.

Students who change majors do so because of
changing interests or because they are forced
to face "institutional realities." Major-
changers often drift without recognition or
advising. Many students are able to make an
otherwise difficult transition into another
academic area if they are given special
curricular and career advising. An innovative
program for helping these students identify,
explore, and decide on alternative educational
and career directions is described.

147.   Gordon, V.N. (1981). The undecided
student: A developmental perspective.
Personnel and Guidance Journal, 59, 433-439.

Student indecision regarding careers and
college majors has been the focus of research
studies for more than 50 years. These studies
have indicated few significant differences
between undecided and decided students. This
article describes undecided students as
normal, growing, predictable individuals in

various stages of vocational and cognitive
development. It also discusses the use of
developmental concepts in academic advising,
career counseling, and teaching.

148.   Gordon, V.N. (1984). The undecided
college student: An academic and career
advising challenge. Springfield, IL: Charles
C. Thomas.

The way that academic advisers, counselors,
faculty, and administrators can help undecided
college students set and implement educational
and career goals is described. The focus is
on a developmental advising approach and
career development concepts. Origins of
indecision, categories of undecided students,
alternative advising, and model programs for
counseling and advising students are
considered, with attention to program
components, delivery systems, administrative
concerns, individual and group advising
techniques, adviser strategies and training
and program evaluation. A special section on
major-changers is included.

149.   Larson, L.M., Heppner, P.P., Ham, T.,
& Dugan, K. (1988). Investigating multiple
subtypes of career indecision through cluster
analysis. Journal of Counseling Psychology,
35, 439-446.

The primary purpose of this study was to
examine and to describe possible subtypes of
undecided students through cluster analysis.
Eighty-seven undecided and twenty-six decided
students were individually interviewed and
completed four instruments on career planning
and career solving. The cluster analysis
revealed four distinct subtypes of undecided
students: planless avoiders; informed
indecisives; confident but uninformed; and
uninformed.

150.   Lewallen, W. (1993). The impact of being "undecided" on college-student persistence. Journal of College Student Development, 34, 103-112.

Using the CIRP longitudinal database, this study examined the persistence of students who were undecided about a major and career direction. Undecided students have been called a "high-risk" group in some of the retention literature. This study found that, contrary to previous research, being undecided was not associated with persistence. The differences are attributed to methodology since previous studies concentrated on the single student characteristic of being undecided and did not control for potentially biasing variables known to be associated with persistence.

151.   Lucas, M.S., & Epperson, D.L. (1990). Types of vocational undecidedness: A replication and refinement. Journal of Counseling Psychology, 37, 382-388.

This article suggests that vocational undecidedness may be conceptualized more productively if treated as a multivariate phenomenon. In this study, students undecided on career options completed a battery of personality questionnaires. Results of ten of these variables were clustered and analyzed to determine the subtypes. To determine degrees of difference between groups, MANOVA was performed on the variables not included in the cluster. Analysis suggesting some degree of validity of the process, types and expected relevant behaviors are described.

152.   Newman, J.L., Fuqua, D.R., & Minger, C. (1990). Further evidence for the use of career subtypes in defining career status. Career Development Quarterly, 39, 178-188.

In this study, four groups of career-decided
students differentiated by the level of
comfort they reported with their career
choices and two groups of career-undecided
students differentiated by the level of the
problem they perceived their indecision to be,
were compared using three measures of career
status and two measures of anxiety.
Generally, the results seriously challenged
the use of decided versus undecided groupings
in defining career status and suggest that
many career-decided students may benefit from
career intervention. Further investigation of
career subtypes, examining both quantitative
and qualitative dimensions of career status is
recommended.

153.   Salomone, P.R., & McKenna, P. (1982).
Difficult career counseling cases: Unrealistic
vocational aspirations. Personnel and
Guidance Journal, 60, 283-286.

Career counselors are occasionally stymied by
the tenacity with which some clients retain
their unrealistic vocational aspirations.
This article focuses on the perceptual
distortions of both clients and counselors and
reviews the contribution of such distortions
to unrealistic vocational aspirations. The
authors also provide several suggestions for
dealing with unrealistic aspirations and for
assisting clients to develop a balanced
perception of reality.

154.   Serling, D.A., & Betz, N.E. (1990).
Development and evaluation of a measure of
fear of commitment. Journal of Counseling
Psychology, 37, 91-97.

The purpose of this series of studies was to
examine the utility of fear of commitment in
understanding the differences between career
undecidedness versus more complicated and
chronic career indecisiveness. Undecided and

decided college students were targeted on the
basis of the hypothesis that educational
indecision comprises a cognitive and
behavioral pattern that is related to career
indecision and may be related to career
indecisiveness. Results revealed that fear of
commitment was related, as predicted, to both
state and trait anxiety and to self-esteem and
was also found to be significantly higher in
undecided versus decided college students.
Implications for the understanding of career
indecisiveness are discussed.

155.   Steele, G.E., Kennedy, G.J., &
Gordon, V.N. (1993). The retention of major-
changers: A longitudinal study. <u>Journal</u> <u>of</u>
<u>College</u> <u>Student</u> <u>Development,</u> <u>34,</u> 58-62.

An important group of students are those
forced to change their academic majors because
of oversubscription or selective admissions.
A longitudinal study shows the effects of a
specially designed advising program to assist
these students in their transition from one
major to another. The special advising
program consists of intrusive individual and
group counseling, workshops to help students
explore alternatives, special academic and
career library resources, and a credit course.
After five years, students in this program
were compared with a randomly selected group
and a cohort group with the same
characteristics. It was found that students
who received the special advising had better
retention and graduation rates, and their
choice of major was more stable upon leaving
the program than the other two groups.

156.   Theophilides, C., Terenzini, P.T., &
Lorang, W. (1984). Freshman and sophomore
experiences and change in major field. <u>Review</u>
<u>of</u> <u>Higher</u> <u>Education,</u> <u>7,</u> 261-278.

Entering freshmen at a large, selective public

university completed the Cooperative
institutional Research Program "Student
Information Form." A follow-up questionnaire
was completed the two successive years. About
one-fourth of the respondents did not change
their major during the two-year period whereas
45 percent changed their major in both years.
Another 15 percent changed their major in the
first year and the final 15 percent changed
their major in the second year.

Chapter 4

Culturally Diverse Students

A. African American Students

157.   Astin, A.W. (1990). The black undergraduate: Current status and trends in the characteristics of freshmen. Los Angeles: University of California, Higher Education Research Institute, Graduate School of Education. (ERIC Document Reproduction Service No. ED 325 043)

This report presents a national profile of black college freshmen in 1990. The study focuses on a wide variety of characteristics of black college freshmen. Major findings include: 1) black students reported lower family incomes and educational level than white students; 2) black college freshmen have experienced declining access to financial aid in the form of federal grants and have been forced to rely more on student loans; 3) low tuition was a major factor in black students' decision about which college to attend; 4) black freshmen continue to be less well-prepared for college compared to their white counterparts; and 5) career choices of black students do not reflect preferences for careers in the sciences or college teaching.

158.   Bernstein, A., Marchese, T.J.,
Newman, F., & Edgerton, R. (Eds.) (1987).
Blacks in higher education: The climb toward
equality. [Special Issue] Change, 19, 14-60.

The feature articles in this issue focus on
the current status of black access to higher
education. The first article examines current
data on black high school graduation rates and
enrollment in higher education, noting the
impact of factors such as financial aid
availability and the option of military
enlistment. The second article presents
preliminary data from a study of ten
universities with a history of success in
graduating minority students. Additional
topics covered include the choice that black
students have to make between predominantly
white and historically black institutions, the
impact of standardized tests on black
students, and the need for black teachers in
primary and secondary education.

159.   Bynum, A.S. (1991). Black
student/white counselor: Developing effective
relationships. (2nd ed.). Indianapolis, IN:
Alexandria Books, Inc.

When students are culturally or racially
different from their counselors, advising and
counseling can be weakened. A counselor's
limited cultural awareness will not produce a
effective interpersonal relationship.
Empathic understanding and good knowledge of a
client generally will provide a springboard
for good relationship development when the
counselor and the client are of different
racial backgrounds. This book provides a
historical and cultural overview of the black
student's world, and illustrates how to use
this knowledge to enhance relationships
between white counselors and black clients.
Specific strategies and techniques are
outlined. A holistic approach that recognizes

all aspects of students' lives, including the
influence of special family ties and the
impact of black culture and tradition, should
be used. Suggestions are offered for changing
attitudes and behavior that evidence the
racial bias that exists to some degree in all
white counselors. Appendices present a
bibliography, a black history/life reading
list, a community resource list, and a
holistic process for academic counseling.

160.   Clayton, B., & Lewis, W.M. (1984).
Some resources for advising minority students:
CESHEP, black colleges and black members of
NACADA. NACADA Journal, 4, 83-88.

The college campus is a microcosm of society,
and it must provide minority and majority
students with academic advising so that their
maximum potentials as individuals and as
members of the total community may be
realized. A bibliography for background and
understanding of the black experience is
provided.

161.   Jackson, G.A. (1984). Helpful hints
for advising and counseling minority students
in predominantly white colleges and
universities. (ERIC Document Reproduction
Service No. ED 255 162)

Advice about advising and counseling minority
students at predominantly white colleges, and
data about the enrollment and majors of
minorities are provided. Included are a list
of hints concerning: personal relations and
student retention, educational development,
financial assistance, and career planning. A
list of words and phrases that offend minority
students is also provided, along with a
checklist questionnaire to help educators
identify behavior they may display in and out
of the classroom that is interpreted by
students as prejudicial, hostile, and

discriminatory. Attention is also directed to
ways that high school counselors and college
admissions staff can help students maximize
their chances of entering and succeeding in
college; recommended courses for college-
bound students for grades 9-12; and
information on federal student aid programs.
Recommendations for college administrators are
also included.

162.   Post, P., Stewart, M.A., & Smith,
P.L. (1991). Self-efficacy, interest, and
consideration of math/science and non-
math/science occupations among Black freshmen.
Journal of Vocational Behavior, 38, 179-186.

Traditionally, black students, compared to
whites, have been underrepresented in math and
science careers. Some of the reasons,
according to the authors, include childhood
experiences, degree of encouragement, academic
preparation, and a paucity of role models.
This study examined the effects of gender,
self-efficacy, and interest on black
freshmen's consideration of math/science and
non-math/science careers. The most
significant result was that more factors
influenced the freshmen's consideration of
math/science occupations than non-math/science
occupations. Black freshmen in this study did
not consider their abilities to complete the
academic work associated with the occupation
or their ability to perform the task in the
occupation when making an initial career
decision. Men considered a broader array of
career choices, which included both
math/science and non-math/science options.
Men also reported greater confidence, self-
efficacy, interest, and consideration of
math/science occupations than women. The
authors suggest that a counseling/advising
goal may be reducing traditional gender
differences by increasing the confidence and
self-efficacy interest in and consideration

for math/science careers among black females.

163.   Roper, L.D., & McKenzie, A. (1988).
Academic advising: A developmental model for
black student athletes. NASPA Journal, 26,
91-98.

This article presents a model for a
comprehensive developmental approach to
advising black athletes. Although the program
was developed for black students, the
developmental issues addressed may be applied
to all athletes. Educators and administrators
most directly responsible for student athletes
must be willing and able to develop individual
and group interventions that respond
adequately to their educational needs.

164.   Wright, D.J. (Ed.) (1987).
Responding to the needs of today's minority
students. New Directions for Student Services
No. 38. San Francisco: Jossey-Bass.

This sourcebook offers suggestions,
considerations, and methods for developing
programs and services to enhance the
recruitment and retention of minority
students. The first chapter reviews the
historical background of minority student
involvement in higher education including the
impact of state/territorial acquisitions,
World War II, the civil rights movement,
changes in immigration patterns, federal
involvement, and models, theories, and
strategies of student development. Subsequent
chapters focus on white minority peer
interaction, the changing needs of black
students, and the special needs of other
minority students. Emphasis is placed on
the distinguishing characteristics and needs
of the various minority groups as well as
their common needs.

B. **Asian American Students**

165.   Asian and Pacific Americans: Behind
the myths. (1989).   Change, 22, 12-63.

The first article in this special issue traces
the changing image of Asian Americans and its
implications.   A box essay refutes the
argument that Asian Americans are a model
minority.   The next article summarizes the
demographic backgrounds of the largest Asian
American ethnic groups.   The following article
presents interviews with six Asian American
students attending six diverse colleges and
universities.   Additional articles discuss the
debate about Asian American admissions, the
need to empower Asian American faculty
members, the absence of a solid audience for
Asian American arts and literature, and the
role of Asian American studies in countering
cultural domination by the existing Euro-
American knowledge base taught in American
colleges.

166.   Atkinson, D.R., Whiteley, S., & Gim,
R.H. (1990).   Asian American acculturation and
preferences for help providers.   Journal of
College Student Development, 31, 155-161.

This study sought to determine if Asian-
American students' preferences for help
providers are a function of their level of
acculturation.   It also speculated that there
would be an inverse relationship between level
of acculturation and ratings given older
relatives and older members of the community
as sources of help.   It found that level of
acculturation for Asian-American college
students was significantly related to ratings
of counselors/psychologists as help providers.
"Asian-identified" students gave the highest
rating to counselors/psychologists as a help
provider, while western-identified respondents
gave the lowest rating.   The relationship
between level of acculturation and ratings for
older family members was not supported.   The

authors suggest that acculturation plays a
significant role in determining to whom Asian
Americans will turn for help with a problem.
Contrary to earlier findings, the values of
more traditional Asian Americans do not seem
to be antithetical to seeing a counselor for
help with a personal problem.

167.   Chew, C.A., & Ogi, A.Y. (1987).
Asian American college student perspectives.
In D.J. Wright (Ed.), Responding to the needs
of today's minority students. New Directions
for Student Services, no. 38. San Francisco:
Jossey-Bass.

This chapter discusses the learning, social,
and emotional needs of Asian American college
students and portrays multicultural existence
as a challenge for practitioners working with
them. Several strategies for developing
programs and services are recommended. To
reach full potential, practitioners must
challenge themselves to reach Asian American
students and reflect their culture's rich
diversity in high quality programs and
services.

168.   Fernandez, M.S. (1988). Issues in
counseling Southeast Asian students. Journal
of Multicultural Counseling and Development,
16, 157-166.

This article seeks to delineate which factors
bring about culture shock for southeast
Asians, that is, people from Burma, Cambodia,
Indonesia, Laos, Malaysia, Philippines,
Singapore, Thailand, and Vietnam. This
article examines the basic assumption of
counseling in light of the Asian culture. In
order to understand culture shock, one must
first delineate cultural differences. Some of
the differences that are covered in this
article include time orientation, role of the
family and its individual members, value

systems, social behavior, and student
expectations.

169.   Gim, R.H., Atkinson, D.R., & Soo,
J.K. (1991). Asian American acculturation,
counselor ethnicity and cultural sensitivity,
and ratings of counselors. Journal of
Counseling Psychology, 38, 57-62.

The ethnicity and cultural sensitivity of a
counselor were examined as they influenced
Asian American students' perceptions of
counselor credibility and cultural competence.
Results suggested that counselor ethnicity and
cultural sensitivity, participant
acculturation, and participant gender all play
a role in how Asian American students perceive
the cultural competence and credibility of a
counselor. Women perceive a culture-sensitive
Asian-American counselor as being most
culturally competent, whereas men perceive a
cultural sensitive Caucasian American
counselor as most culturally competent. Low-
acculturated subjects gave their lowest
credibility ratings to the culture-blind
Caucasian American counselor. Overall, Asian
Americans perceived a racially similar
counselor who is culture-sensitive as being
most culturally competent and credible.
Counselors need to be aware of the role
culture may play in clients' problems and how
student perceptions of the counseling process
may be culturally influenced.

170.   Hsia, J. (1988). Asian Americans in
higher education and at work. Hillsdale, NJ:
Laurence Erlbaum.

An introduction to this volume presents
historical backgrounds and demographic
descriptions of Asian American students today.
The following chapters include 1) the
developed academic ability of Asian Americans
based on standardized test scores, 2) the

academic achievement and extra-curricular
activities of college bound Asian Americans,
3) the historic and current situation of Asian
Americans in terms of their aspiration and
access to and enrollment in higher education,
4) overall achievement of Asian Americans in
the United States postsecondary educational
institutions, 5) career directions of Asian
Americans, and 6) a summary of findings and
discussion of the implications and
recommendations for higher education.

171.   Li, V.H. (1988). Asian
discrimination: Fact or fiction? College
Board Review, 149, 20.

Some college admissions officers and selection
processes are insensitive to Asian American
conditions and issues. Not all Asian Americans
are high achievers who are well established in
American society. An important factor to be
remembered is that Asian American students
come from a large number of countries with
highly distinct cultures, languages and
histories. This article suggests that the
economically disadvantaged Asian American
students require a greater share of admissions
officers' attention and care than do the
overachievers at the top of the scale.
Recommendations are presented and discussed.

C. **Hispanic American Students**

172.   Attinasi, L.C. (1989). Getting in:
Mexican American's perception of university
attendance and the implications for freshman
year persistence. Journal of Higher
Education, 60, 247-277.

Inductive analysis of in-depth, open-ended
interviews of persisting and non-persisting
Mexican American university students yielded
two conceptual schemas, corresponding to pre-
and post-matriculation attitudinal and

behavioral patterns, for interpreting their
perceptions of college-going experiences.
These schemas formed the bases for examining
the sociopsychological context of freshman
year persistence decisions.

173.   McKenna, T., & Oritz, F.I. (1988).
The broken web: The educational experience of
Hispanic American women. Encino, CA:
Floricanto Press.

In this volume, various authors document an
educational situation that undermines the
ability of Hispanic American women to fulfill
their potential by inadequately attending to
their gender-specific problems. Two prologue
articles assess the status of the education of
Hispanic American women and the institutional
responsibility of providing educational
experience for them. A context and critique
section discusses the interdependency of
educational institutions and cultural norms.

174.   Quevedo-Garcia, E.L. (1987).
Facilitating the development of Hispanic
college students. In D.J. Wright (Ed.)
Responding to the needs of today's minority
students. New Directions for Student
Services, No. 38. San Francisco: Jossey-
Bass.

While U.S. Hispanics are purported to be among
the fastest growing population groups in the
nation, their growth will be realized when
colleges devise innovative approaches to
Hispanic student programs and services. If
practitioners are to be successful in
structuring environments that will help
Hispanic college students develop to their
full potential as individuals, they must fully
understand and appreciate the various
cultural, economic, social and political
backgrounds that these students bring with
them to the campuses.

175.   Rendon, L.I., & Nora, A. (1989).   A
synthesis and application of research on
Hispanic students in community colleges.
Community College Review, 17, 17-24.

According to many studies, problems for
Hispanic students originate at the pre-college
level, where Hispanic graduation rates are
also low. Overall, Hispanic students with
strong institutional and goal commitments are
the most likely to persist in their education.
Community colleges should provide counseling
and advisement, ideally involving faculty
members, to help Hispanic students discover
suitable career and educational goals.   In
addition, financial aid counseling should be
made available to Hispanic students,
preferably beginning in high school.

D. **Native American Students**

176.   American Indian voices in higher
education. (1991).   Change, 23, 4-46.

This special report features the Native
American student in higher education, and the
many issues that are involved in their college
career. Topics of the various articles in
this report include a look at the history of
cultural conflict, the Native American student
in the college curriculum, a model for a
college intervention program, a look at Indian
education in Minnesota, ways of empowering the
students, and the final article on educating
to Americanize.

177.   Amiotte, L., & Allen, T. (1988).   The
four-year community college: Tribal college,
some lessons in success for Indian students in
college. (ERIC Document Reproduction Service
No. 305 101)

Drawing from the experience of Oglala Lakota
College (OLC) in South Dakota, this paper

points to the philosophical and operational
changes colleges and universities must make if
they truly desire to recruit and retain
significant numbers of minority students. The
first section discusses the philosophical
bases of tribal colleges. The next section
highlights recommendations from a variety of
sources with respect to methods of recruiting
and retaining minority students. Concluding
comments stress the importance to minority
success of incorporating service to minorities
as part of a college's mission, of having a
physical presence in the minority community,
of developing a supportive climate, of
maintaining a cultural base, and of committing
financial resources.

178.   Change trendlines: Native Americans
and higher education - new mood of optimism.
(1990) Change, 22, 27-30.

An example of a tribal college is presented.
Native Americans can succeed given the chance
to study in an environment that respects their
culture, provides extra support, and given
adequate financial assistance. Non-tribal
colleges can look to the tribal model to
strengthen their own outreach programs.
Moreover, the federal government can encourage
the tribal colleges' success by funding them
fully. Only through such measures can large
numbers of Native Americans earn their degrees
and help determine and improve both their own
fate and that of their people.

179.   Hornett, D. (1989). The role of
faculty in cultural awareness and retention of
American Indian college students. Journal of
American Indian Education, 29, 12-18.

The attrition rate of minority students at
institutions of higher learning continues to
be a major problem. Retention of minority
students, especially at predominantly white

institutions, has been discouraging.
Educators, concerned with the high drop out
rate, continue to look for reasons, as well as
solutions to the problem. This article
focuses on a one very important asset of
colleges and universities that is often
ignored - the faculty.

180.   Johnson, M.E., & Lashley, K.H.
(1989). Influence of Native Americans'
cultural commitment on preferences for
counselor ethnicity and expectations about
counseling. Journal of Multicultural
Counseling and Development, 17, 115-122.

In this study, Native Americans completed a
questionnaire that assessed demographic
characteristics, level of commitment to the
Native American and Anglo American cultures
and expectations concerning the counseling
process. Analysis revealed that the students
who reported strong commitment to the Native
American culture also reported greater
involvement in tribal activities. In
addition, students who were strongly committed
to the Native American culture showed a
greater preference for an ethnically similar
counselor and expected counselors to show
higher levels of facilitativeness, nurturance,
and expertise than did their counterparts.

181.   Lin, R.L. (1990). Perception of
family background and personal characteristics
among Indian college students. Journal of
American Indian Education, 29, 19-26.

In this study, Native American students
responded to a questionnaire about their
family backgrounds and academic performance.
The students' family backgrounds were
classified as traditional or modern on the
basis of the responses. In five areas of
academic performance, the students from
traditional family backgrounds had higher GPAs

and spent more time doing homework, whereas the students from modern families cared more about professors' opinions and skipped more classes. T tests further revealed that the students from modern families were less likely to feel that their education conflicted with family values.

182.   McWhirter, J.J., & Ryan, C.A. (1991). Counseling the Navajos: Cultural understanding. Journal of Multicultural Counseling and Development, 19, 74-82.

Counselors who work with Native Americans might profit from greater insight into their clients by recognizing their basic life style and the effect it has on children, adults, and family units. The purpose of this article was to identify several issues that seem important in counseling Navajos. Some issues may also be appropriate to nonreservation Native Americans, especially those whose roots are tied to the reservation.

183.   Oppelt, N.T. (1989). Cultural values and behaviors common among tribal American Indians: A resource for student service administrators. NASPA Journal, 26, 167-174.

This article discusses how American Indians of today are as diverse in their values, attitudes, and behaviors as any other race of people. They are also stereotyped and misunderstood by most non-Indians. By acknowledging commonly held Indian values and beliefs, student personnel workers can facilitate the Indian's development as a bi-cultural person.

184.   Rindone, P. (1988). Achievement motivation and academic achievement of Native American students. Journal of American Indian Education, 28, 1-8.

This study examined the backgrounds of Navajo individuals who had completed at least a four-year college degree, in an attempt to identify those characteristics that were "most influential" in their pursuit of a college degree. The findings indicated that the family (as measured through the stability of traditional values) was the key to the academic success of these high achieving Navajos.

185.   Wells, R.N. (1989). A survey of American Indian students. (ERIC Document Reproduction Service No. ED 311 778)

A survey was conducted to obtain more reliable data on Native Americans in higher education and to ascertain the factors contributing to their success and failure in college. Findings included the following: 1) as a group, American colleges provide relatively few data for Native Americans and do not have programs aimed at breaking down specific barriers to Native American achievement; 2) retention and matriculation rates for Native American students are low; 3) although institutional support programs and pre-college intervention programs have increased, the Native American student's financial and personal or family problems continue to be roadblocks to academic success; 4) the major barriers to higher education are economic difficulties, inadequate college preparation, and difficulties adjusting to college. Tutoring programs, developmental and remedial courses, structured counseling, and pre-college orientation are recommended.

186.   Wright, B. (1989). Tribally controlled community colleges: An assessment of student satisfaction. Community/Junior College Quarterly of Research and Practice, 13, 119-128.

A survey was conducted of Native American
students who attended seven tribal community
colleges. The majority chose to attend a
tribal college because other colleges were
located too far from home. The students cited
a number of job-related reasons for enrolling
in tribal colleges: preparing for a new
career, improving job skills, opportunity for
advancement, discovering a vocational
interest, and earning a vocational
certificate. Most of the students agreed that
the tribal college had been moderately
successful in helping them to obtain their
goals.

E. International Students

187.   Dalili, F. (1982). Roles and
responsibilities of international student
advisors and counselors in the United States.
(ERIC Document reproduction Service No. ED 226
658)

The separate but complementary roles of the
international student advisor and counselor
are discussed, and foreign student personnel
services are addressed. It is suggested that
the increasing number of international
students indicates a need for a full-time
foreign student advisor. International
students need assistance in admissions and
orientation, information about institutional
facilities and services, and understanding of
laws regarding aliens. Foreign students are
often unfamiliar with American society and
aspects of university life, including academic
programming, registration procedures, and
financial aid, housing, and health services.
An international student counselor should
facilitate the student's adjustments.

188.   Deressa, B., & Beavers, I. (1986).
Academic and non- academic needs of
international students. Journal of College

Student _Personnel,_ _20,_ 411-416.

The purposes of this study were to identify academic and nonacademic needs of international students enrolled in a midwestern college of home economics and to make recommendations for educational experiences more meaningful for students. A needs statement inventory included academic needs, housing needs, social and personal problems, cultural values, and financial needs. Significant differences were found between regions of the world from which students came, academic major, intensive English studied in the United States, and effects of the English language when taking examinations.

189.   Leong, F.T.L., & Sedlacek, W.E. (1986). A comparison of international and U.S. students' preferences for help sources. _Journal_ _of_ _College_ _Student_ _Personnel,_ _27,_ 426-430.

In this study, the authors investigated what sources of help would be used by international students for emotional-social and educational-vocational problems and compared these findings with those for U.S. students. International students were more likely than students from the United States to prefer faculty members and counselors and less likely to prefer friends for help with all kinds of problems.

190.   Pyle, K.R. (Ed.) (1986). _Guiding_ _the_ _development_ _of_ _foreign_ _students._ _New_ _Directions_ _for_ _Student_ _Services:_ _No. 36._ San Francisco: Jossey-Bass.

This sourcebook presents several perspectives on understanding foreign students for student affairs professionals. Seven chapters cover the following topics: ways in which **84** professionals can encourage interactions between foreign and non-foreign students; the causes of difficulties and conflicts for foreign students, and an outline of their demographic make-up; guidelines for admissions offices and student affairs departments on the recruiting and admission of foreign students; the ways of integrating foreign students into the campus community; counseling, advising, and the specific needs of foreign students; review of the current literature on foreign students; and trends, issues, and recommendations for the foreign student.

191.   Wherly, B. (1988). Cultural diversity from an international perspective, Part II. Journal of Multicultural Counseling and Development, 16, 3-15.

Counselors must recognize that many international students are reluctant to share problems outside the family, attach different meaning to nonverbal behavior, and have specific expectations regarding formality, advice giving, talking and listening, and problems solving. With these types of problems in mind, foreign students' advisors may need to make adaptations for this unique population of students.

Chapter 5

Adviser Training

192.   Bostaph, C., & Moore, M. (1980). Training academic advisors: A developmental strategy. Journal of College Student Personnel, 21, 45-50.

Five academic advising functions are the focus for training suggestions. The authors recommend financial reward for advisors, as well as positive feedback, recognition, and staff support, based on the tenet that advising plays a critical role in retention and the promotion of the institution's image to prospective students. The authors also suggest training programs which use interview simulations as well as observation of working advisers. They also recommend an in-service program which would have an internal as well as an external development component. Developmental theory underlies this strategy.

193.   Boulet, M.M., et al. (1990). Advisor system: Conception of an intervention module. Computers and Education, 14, 17-29.

This article discusses intervention modules for use with computer software and describes the development of an intelligent adviser system, or help system, to aid a user in

developing a conceptual data model using the
entity-relation method and graphics software.
Knowledge acquisition is discussed, and an
example of an adviser intervention is given.

194.   Carberry, J.D. (1986). Applying
cognitive developmental theory in the advising
setting. NACADA Journal, 6, 13-18.

Advisers need to be familiar with student
needs and experiences. Cognitive
developmental theory can enhance the "art of
teaching" and understanding the cognitive
stages of student development can help the
adviser appreciate a student's perspective.
Cognitive theory is translated into useful
advising strategies.

195.   Chan, D.Y., & Cochran, J.K. (1988).
Using expert-system shells for graduate
student advising. Engineering
Education, 78, 310-312.

A computer system to help advise industrial
and management systems engineering students is
described. The article discusses the expert
system, "Personal Consultant" that was used in
developing the overall process.

196.   Coll, K.M., & House, R.M. (1991).
Empirical implications for the training and
professional development of community college
counselors. Community College Review, 19, 43-
52.

This article describes a study of the
appropriate major and professional development
needs of community college counselors,
highlighting survey responses from counselor
educators and student services co-workers.
Results of the survey present counselor
duties/functions, and perceptions of counselor
role conflict and role ambiguity.

197.   Duke, W., & Moxley, L.S. (1988).
Academic interface: A suggested approach.
NASPA Journal, 26, 124-128. A retreat format
was used to identify specific ways in which
student affairs professionals and faculty can
develop shared goals. Actions taken as a
result of the retreat are listed, including
financial rewards to outstanding faculty
advisers and a training program for academic
advisers.

198.   Ender, S.C., & Winston, R.B. (1982).
Training allied professional academic
advisors. In R.B. Winston, S.C. Ender, and
T.K. Miller (Eds.), Developmental approaches
to academic advising: New directions for
student services, No. 17. San Francisco:
Jossey-Bass.

This chapter presents the essential skills and
competencies that all advisers must possess if
they are to offer truly effective academic
advising. The authors identify eleven
components and outline goals and outcome
objectives for each component. Critical
issues to be addressed in a training program
are discussed.

199.   Enhancing academic advising skills:
A resource manual for staff development.
(1981). Milwaukee: University of Wisconsin
Counseling and Advising Network. (ERIC
Document Reproduction Service No. ED 235 699)

A handbook describes four main topics to cover
in adviser training: philosophies, goals,
policies, and procedures of the university.
Also included are job-specific knowledge of
each school or division, ethical concerns, and
advising skills and techniques. Ethical
concerns covered include student records,
sexual harassment, and the adviser's anecdotal
records. The section on advising skills and
techniques includes establishing rapport,

nonverbal communication, active listening,
information giving, and problem solving.
Student assessment and monitoring academic
performance are discussed.

200.   Ford, J., & Ford, S.S. (1990).
Producing a comprehensive academic advising
handbook. Houston, TX: Houston Baptist
University. (ERIC Document Reproduction
Service No. ED 339 435)

A comprehensive academic advising handbook is
the cornerstone of a well-developed,
implemented academic advising program. The
authors detail seven steps in handbook
development: making the commitment, assigning
responsibility, determining objectives and
purposes of the handbook, determining content,
organization of the handbook, presentation of
the handbook (typing, binding, etc.), and
updating. Additional notes and suggestions
for training for its use are included.

201.   Gelwick, B.P. (1974). Training
faculty to do career advising. Personnel and
Guidance Journal, 53, 214-217.

A study of a project to train faculty advisers
to include lifelong career guidance in their
academic advising is described. Based upon
several assumptions from vocational
development theory, deliberate psychological
education, and group dynamic theory, the
program had a preponderance of positive
responses from faculty, trainers, and
advisees. An outline of the program is
included.

202.   Gordon, V.N. (1980). Training
academic advisers: Content and method.
Journal of College Student Personnel, 21, 334-
339.

Academic adviser training is a vital component

of an effective advising program. Academic
advisers need to be trained in fundamental
concepts and functions, which are the same
regardless of the setting. Five essential
elements of an adviser training program are
described. They include: the academic
advising process, student characteristics and
development, career development advising,
campus resources, and the college environment.
Objectives and evaluation methods are also
discussed.

203.   Gordon, V.N. (1982). Training future
academic advisers: One model of a pre-service
approach. NACADA Journal, 2, 35-40.

A graduate-level course to introduce future
faculty, staff, counselors, and administrators
to the role of advising and the adviser in
higher education is described. The course
includes segments on organizational advising
models and delivery systems, techniques and
resources, special problems and populations,
and career advising. Communication skills are
emphasized.

204.   Gordon, V.N. (1984). Training
professional and paraprofessional advisers.
In R. Winston, T.K. Miller, S.C. Ender, T.
Grites, and Associates (Eds.), Developmental
academic advising. San Francisco: Jossey-
Bass.

This chapter provides a complete description
for developing an effective adviser training
program which includes determining the need,
obtaining administrative support, setting
objectives, identifying program content and
topics, selecting appropriate strategies and
methods, evaluating the program, and future
planning. A section on training
paraprofessional advisers is also included.

205.   Gordon, V.N. (1992). Adviser

development and training. In V.N. Gordon,
Handbook of academic advising. Westport, CT:
Greenwood Press.

This chapter provides an overview of adviser
training issues and methods. Different
aspects of training components such as
establishing objectives, content, methods and
techniques, training location, and evaluation
are described. The issue of rewards is
addressed. A training committee is suggested
as a vehicle for insuring adviser training is
responsive to campus and student needs. In-
service and pre-service approaches are
outlined.

206.   Grites, T.J. (1984). Techniques and
tools for improving advising. NACADA Journal,
4, 55-74.

A sampling of publications, assessment
instruments, institutional resource documents,
campus agencies, and human resources that may
be useful to academic advisers are examined.
In order to be able to select and use these
materials effectively, an adviser training
program is necessary. The training program
enables the advisers to achieve the maximum
potential use of the available advising tools
and resources, and it must include strategies
for introducing them. Participation in such a
program is also
a developmental activity for the advisers.

207.   Kelly, J.J. (1988). Developing the
advising "tool kit." NACADA Journal, 8, 81-84.

Developing an inventory consisting of each and
every item that contributes to a total
advising program is suggested. Since advisers
are becoming increasingly integral to the
entire educational mission of colleges and
universities, an "advising tool kit" or
inventory of important advising materials can

be used to demonstrate to faculty,
administrators and staff how comprehensive,
complex and important advising has become. A
sampling of contents of a "tool kit" is given
which includes bulletins, curriculum guides,
informational brochures, student handbooks,
college and major checklists, orientation
materials, study abroad broad brochures, and
various communications from offices such as
financial aid, career development and
placement, the registrar, and academic
departments.

208.   Keller, M.C. (1988). Adviser
training. In W.R. Habley (Ed.) The status
and future of academic advising. Iowa City,
IA: The American College Testing Program.

In this chapter, the author examines the basic
elements necessary for developing an effective
adviser training program. The need for
programs which incorporate developmental
principles are demonstrated and some of the
key ingredients of such programs are
highlighted. The author presents a model
which provides specific strategies to assist
advisers with implementing developmentally
oriented goals. The chapter concludes with an
overview of some proven adviser training
strategies.

209.   Kishler, T.C. (1985). Developing an
all-university adviser's training program: A
short history of one model. (ERIC Document
Reproduction Service No. ED 261 578)

An inservice training program for advisers
that was implemented at Michigan State
University is discussed. Four primary
ingredients were essential to establish and
sustain the program: financial support and
sponsorship by the central administration, the
identification and authorization of the
administrator to coordinate the endeavor, the

promotion of the enterprise across the
university, and the timely notification of
possible attendees of upcoming adviser
conferences. Meeting topics included:
development and implementation of new
programs, advising for the general education
program, issues in academic advising of
minority students, and advising foreign
students.

210.   Kramer, H.C. (1983). Advising:
Implications for faculty development. NACADA
Journal, 3, 25-31.

A healthy advising program serves as a useful
vehicle for faculty development. An
institution may use the program to develop
faculty skills useful in other contexts than
the individual student's welfare. Advising
programs should endeavor to improve students,
faculty, and the institution.

211.   Kramer, H.C. (1984). Advising the
advisor. NACADA Journal, 4, 41-51.

How advising by faculty may be used as one of
many faculty roles that can help the
institution and the individual faculty member
is described. A dynamic relationship exists
between the development of the individual
faculty, the development of their careers, and
the overall well being of higher education.
Areas covered include 1) the institution's
view of the future, 2) adviser benefits, 3)
adviser incentives, 4) considerations for the
advising coordinator, and 5) implications for
the institution.

212.   Kramer, H.C. (1986). Faculty
development: The advising coordinator's
changing scene. NACADA Journal, 6, 31-42.

Institutional vitality will require
imaginative linking of professional

development of individual faculty with
carefully planned development of academic
programs and institutional policies. Academic
advising is discussed as faculty development.
Faculty anxiety about scholarly production is
described.

213.   Kramer, H.C. (1987) Practicum
training for advisors. (ERIC Document
Reproduction Service No. ED 287 337)

The use of a practicum form of training of
faculty advisers is discussed. Understanding
the advising process may be viewed as a
transaction between master adviser (advising
mentor) and faculty adviser. An understanding
of the interaction between student and faculty
adviser can be replicated. Using the
practicum setting to help advisers is a method
for representing essential features of
advising practice while enabling learners to
experiment at low risk, and vary the pace and
focus of their work. A behavioral change
model is used to critique the applicability of
using a reflective practicum setting in an
adviser training program.

214.   Kramer, H.C., & Gardner, R.E. (1983).
Advising by faculty. (rev. ed.) Washington,
D.C.: National Education Association. (ERIC
Document Reproduction Service No. 235 742)

This booklet may be used individually or as a
training vehicle for faculty advisers. It is
designed to 1) provide a working definition of
advising, 2) describe a theoretical framework
for the process of advising, 3) show with
model conversations the theory in practice, 4)
provide procedures for adviser self-
evaluation, and 5) create a vehicle for
discussion of those issues germane to
advising.

215.   Merta, R.J., et al. (1988).

Simulating culture shock in counselor
trainees: An experiential exercise for cross-
cultural training. Journal of Counseling and
Development, 66, 242-245.

In this article the authors describe a
bipartite learning exercise designed to
increase counselor trainees' sensitivity to
cultural differences. The exercise emphasizes
extending traditional cognitive-focused
multicultural training to include actual
interactions with diverse persons. A two
month follow-up evaluation indicated that
trainees viewed the learning exercise as
valuable. Suggestions are made for infusing
similar experientially based exercises into
other training vehicles.

216.   Milheim, W.D., & Azbell, J.W. (1988,
January). How past research control can aid
in the design of interactive video materials.
Proceedings of Selected Research Papers
presented at the Annual Meeting of the
Association for Educational Communications and
Technology, New Orleans, LA. (ERIC Document
Reproduction Service No. ED 295 652)

This paper examines prior research on learner
control in an effort to apply the findings to
the design of interactive video systems.
Early research on learner control is detailed,
including descriptions of research supporting
learning control or having mixed reactions to
learner control. Alternatives to learner
control are also discussed, including adaptive
control strategies and learner control with
advisement. The effects of learner
characteristics on learner control are
considered, and research that specifically
considers interactive video is detailed.
Suggestions for the effective design of
interactive video materials emphasize the
importance of training, the need for
individualized design, and the effect of

content on learner control and retention.

217.   Moore, C.A, et al (1985).   Advising
the advisors: A preventative intervention
strategy.   Paper presented at the National
Conference of the American College
Personnel Association, Boston, MA.   (ERIC
Document Reproduction Service No. ED 206 614)

Workshops for academic advisers developed by
the university counseling service are
described.   The purposes of the workshop
series designed for faculty and academic
advisers were to: promote collaboration
between student services staff and faculty,
reduce the frustration and burnout reported by
advisers in addressing student concerns for
which they felt unprepared, increase the ease
of referral by adviser to appropriate student
service professionals, and reduce incidents of
poor advising.   Outlines are provided for two
workshops including advising, interviewing and
referral, and choosing majors and careers.
Additional topics for training programs are
also provided.

218.   Peavy, R.V. (1992).   A constructivist
model of training for career counselors.
Journal of Career Development, 18, 215-228.

A survey of new faculty at the end of the year
indicated that they did not feel prepared to
advise.   Sixty-six percent said they needed
training to be better advisers, while 83
percent would have attended adviser training
programs if offered.

219.   Weston, P.K. (1993).   Adviser
training in the community college.   In M.C.
King (Ed.), Academic advising: Organizing and
delivering services for student success, New
Directions for Community Colleges, No. 82.
(pp. 55-61).   San Francisco: Jossey-Bass.

Components of an effective adviser training
program in community colleges are provided
including informational content, conceptual
content, and relational skills. Types of
adviser training programs are given. A model
training outline is offered.

220.   Yerian, J.M., & Miller, T.K. (Eds.)
(1989). Putting the CAS standards to work.
Training manual for the CAS Self Assessment
Guides. Council for the Advancement of
Standards for Student Services/Development
Programs. (ERIC Document Reproduction Service
No. ED 305 547)

These 18 self-assessment guides and training
manual from the Council for the Advancement of
Standards (CAS) for Student Services/
Development Programs, translate the CAS
Standards and Guidelines into a format for
self-study purposes. These training guides
allow an institution to assure compliance with
minimally-acceptable practice, gain an
informed perspective on strengths and
deficiencies, plan for program improvement,
and prepare for review by external evaluators.
The training manual outlines eight steps in
using the guides.

Chapter 6

Career Advising

221.   Althen, G., & Stott, F.W. (1983). Advising and counseling students who have unrealistic academic objectives. <u>Personnel and Guidance Journal, 17,</u> 608-611.

This study explores the motivation of students who have academic or career aspirations that seem beyond their reach and suggests approaches for working with them. The authors give several reasons for this problem, which include personality characteristics, assumptions that there will be exceptions to set standards, external pressures, and cultural differences. Why counselors are less effective with these students is also discussed, as are modes of action and alternatives.

222.   Arbona, C., & Novy, D.M. (1991). Career aspirations and expectations of Black, Mexican American, and White students. <u>Career Development Quarterly, 39,</u> 231-240.

The career aspirations and expectations of Black, Mexican American, and White college freshmen were examined. In addition, students' career expectations were compared to the jobs available in the labor market.

Results suggested that 1) there seemed to be
more gender than ethnic differences in
students' career aspirations and expectations,
2) differences in the career aspirations and
expectations among Mexican American and White
students followed traditional gender patterns,
and 3) with some exceptions, the career
expectations of students resembled the
distribution of jobs in the labor market.

223.   Basta, N. (1991). Major options:
The student's guide to linking college majors
and career opportunities during and after
college. New York: The Stonesong Press.

This book has two parts: a compendium of
majors and a compendium of careers. The first
part describes dozens of the most popular
college majors. Included for each major are:
the numbers of students choosing this major
nationwide for 1983, 1985 and 1988; an
overview of the major which provides general
information such as general course work and
related career opportunities; concentrations
or specializations within the major;
descriptions of courses that would be in the
curriculum; assessment, or examples of
students who have chosen this major; and
specific career options. In the careers
section, job descriptions for many specific
careers are given. Occupational projections
to the year 2000 are provided.

224.   Beatty, J.D., Davis, B., & White, B.
(1983). Open option advising at Iowa State
University: An integrated advising and career
planning model. NACADA Journal, 3, 39-48.

In response to growing numbers of undeclared
majors, a course was developed that included
career exploration and planning in the context
of skill development and information
gathering. Results indicated that increased
declaration of majors increased retention

among those taking the course. It was found that the open option advising model proved to be effective as it: 1) moved open option advising from academic departments to a college advising center; 2) brought faculty to the center to represent general areas; 3) brought faculty and professional advisers together to share their areas of expertise; and 4) used highly trained peer advisers and introduced a career planning/ orientation course.

225.   Blustein, D.L., & Phillips, S.D. (1990). Relation between ego identity status and decision-making styles. Journal of Counseling Psychology, 37, 160-168.

This report examined the proposition that variances in career decision-making are related to identity information process by identifying relations between ego identity status and decision making in college students. Findings support that proposition and suggest stable identity persons use rational and systematic decision-making strategies, while foreclosed identity persons use dependent strategies, and diffusion status persons use intuition and dependent styles.

226.   Fitzpatrick, J.L., & Silverman, T. (1989). Women's selection of careers in engineering: Do traditional-nontraditional differences still exist? Journal of Vocational Behavior, 34, 266-278.

This study compared background and motivational factors of high-achieving college women in engineering, science, and humanities and social sciences of factors affecting career choice. Areas of investigation included family composition and parental characteristics, childhood socialization, sources of support for career choice, and work characteristics. significant differences were

found only in sources of support and work
characteristics. Women choosing traditional
and nontraditional careers are similar when
levels of achievement are comparable. The
continued viability of the traditional-
nontraditional dimension as a measure of
career commitment is discussed.

227.   Fukuyama, M.A., et al. (1988).
Effects of DISCOVER on career self-efficacy
and decision making of undergraduates. Career
Development Quarterly, 37, 56-62.

This study addressed the impact of DISCOVER, a
computerized career guidance system, on career
self-efficacy and decision making among
college undergraduates. Results indicated
that DISCOVER had positive effect on both
career self-efficacy and career decision
making.

228.   Gianakos, I., & Subich, L.M. (1988).
Student sex and sex role in relation to
college major choice. The Career Development
Quarterly, 26, 259-268.

This study examined the economic ramifications
of sex segregation in the workplace and the
suggestion that the origin of the male-female
wage differential in the divergent career
choices of the sexes. The research sought to
provide knowledge regarding how both sex and
sex role may be related to the college major
choices of a broad sample of undergraduates.
The Holland interest typology was used to
classify majors into categories, thus
providing a theoretical framework for
understanding sex and sex roles in career
choice.

229.   Gordon, V.N. (1992). Career
advising. In V. Gordon, Handbook of Academic
Advising (pp. 71-85). Westport, CT: Greenwood
Press.

Career advising is an important area of
expertise for academic advisers since many
students relate academic major choice to
career decisions. This chapter discusses the
career advising process, elements in career
planning, and the changing workplace. Career
advising of undecided students is also
discussed. Practical suggestions are
included.

230.   Gordon, V.N., Cascarelli, W.C., &
Sears, S.J. (1986). Comparative assessments
of individual differences in learning and
career decision making. Journal of College
Student Personnel, 27, 233-241.

This study investigated whether there are
unique and common elements between Johnson's
(1978) theory and other related theories of
decision making and learning among college
students exploring academic and occupational
alternatives. Results indicated that there
are some common elements in the way students
approach learning and career decision making
along with some differences.

231.   Groccia, J.E., & Harrity, M.B.
(1991). A major selection program: A
proactive retention and enrichment program for
undecided freshmen. Journal of College Student
Development, 32, 178-179.

This article describes the Major Selection
Program (MSP) which was initiated to provide
an organized, coordinated and integrated
series of services to assist freshmen with
choosing a major. The underlying goal of the
MSP was to enable undergraduate students to
make reasoned, informed choices of major. The
components of the MSP are: the MSP seminar, a
career resource library, and the Professional-
In-Action program.

232.   Harren, V.A. (1979). A model of

decision making for college students. <u>Journal</u> <u>of</u> <u>Vocational</u> <u>Behavior,</u> <u>14,</u> 119-133.

This classic article presents a model of career decision making which focuses on the typical undergraduate college student. The model includes: a delineation of the internal psychological process of decision making; characteristics of the decision maker; and specification of immediate or anticipated environmental factors influencing decision making. The model is intended to provide a conceptual framework for assessment of student needs, designing counseling and educational interventions, and for generating empirically testable hypotheses.

233.   Healy, C.C., & Mourton, D.L. (1987). The relationship of career exploration, college jobs, and grade point average. <u>Journal</u> <u>of</u> <u>College</u> <u>Student</u> <u>Personnel,</u> <u>28,</u> 28-33.

This study uses path analysis to explore whether a theoretical sequence would account for the relation of career-related variables with one another and with grade point average. Path analysis suggested that college jobs mediated the effects of anxiety, career development skills, and reading ability on grade point averages at a community college.

234.   Johnson, R.H. (1978). Individual styles of decision making: A theoretical model for counseling. <u>Personnel</u> <u>and</u> <u>Guidance</u> <u>Journal,</u> <u>56,</u> 530-536.

The author develops a model that describes and explains the process that individuals use to make decisions. The model centers around how individuals gather information (spontaneously or systematical) and how they analyze it (externally or internally). Combining these two styles results in four decision making

styles: spontaneous external, spontaneous
internal, systematic external, and systematic
internal. The four styles are illustrated
through four vignettes of counselor/client
interactions. Applications for using the
styles in many decision situations are
offered.

235. Katchadourian, H.A., & Boli, J.
(1985). Careerism and intellectualism among
college students. San Francisco: Jossey-
Bass.

This research study was initiated to learn
about the academic experiences of students at
Stanford University in order to enhance the
quality of undergraduate education. The
careerism versus intellectualism controversy
is discussed in the first chapter. Four types
of students: careerists, intellectuals,
strivers, and the unconnected, are described
in the second chapter. Each type is dealt
with in more detail in separate chapters. A
summary of the study's findings and
recommendations for enhancing the
undergraduate experience is discussed in the
final chapter.

236. Kishler, T.C. (1984). Placement data
and advising: Handle with flair but care.
NACADA Journal, 4, 59-65.

This article describes a publication
distributed by the office of placement
services at Michigan State University which
lists by college and major the names of all
students who graduated, and includes degrees
earned the previous academic year. The
publication contains information relevant to
advising students interested in current
employment prospects and trends.

237. Leong, F.T.L. (1991). Career
development attributes and occupational values

of Asian American and White American college
students. <u>Career Development Quarterly, 39,</u>
221-230.

This study examined difference in career
development attributes and occupational values
between Asian and White Americans. Asian
Americans were found to have greater
preferences for dependent decision-making
styles and also a lower level of career
maturity. No differences in vocational
identity were found between the cultural
groups. Asian Americans also placed greater
emphasis on extrinsic and security
occupational value clusters (e.g., making more
money, having a stable, secure future)
relative to White Americans. Counseling and
research implications are discussed.

238.   Lips, H.M. (1992). Gender-and
science-related attitudes as predictors of
college students' academic choices. <u>Journal
of Vocational Behavior, 38,</u> 62-81.

The predictability of gender and science-
related attitudes' were used to examine the
intent to take mathematics and science
courses, intended major, career goals, and the
number of science courses attempted over three
years. Males disagreed more than females that
women can combine scientific careers and
family. Females agreed less than male that
scientists are asocial. Perception of
scientific careers as demanding related
positively to attempting science and
mathematics courses and to selecting
mathematics or science related career goals,
especially for males. Only modest support was
obtained for a relation between women's
beliefs or concerns about combining career and
family responsibilities and their academic and
vocational choices with respect to math and
science.

239.   Marshall, R.P., & Andrews, H.A.
(1990).   Toward a consumer-oriented college
catalog.   Journal of College Admissions, 128,
12-14.

This report describes a new consumer-oriented
approach to the college catalog, the "Catalog
and Decision-Making Guide," which takes a
unique approach to presenting information that
is both useful and helpful in choosing
programs and, ultimately, careers.

240.   McAuliffe, G.J. (1991).   Assessing
and treating barriers to decision making in
career classes.   The Career Development
Quarterly, 40, 82-92.

The author contends that individuals with
personal/emotional barriers to decision making
may receive little help from standard,
information-oriented versions of career
courses offered for credit.   Although research
supports the value of these classes for the
majority of students, some may experience no
progress in decision making.   Four strategies
are offered to individualize interventions.
The author believes that there are many
subgroups within a career class and that these
groups need to be targeted with specific
interventions.

241.   Munski, D.C. (1983).   Maximizing
career oriented academic advising at the
departmental level.   NACADA Journal, 3, 17-20.

A course developed within an academic
department to expose students to discipline-
specific career information and decision
making is described, including course
assignments and student reactions.   A side
benefit has been closer career-oriented
connections between faculty and practitioners.

242.   O'Hare, M.M., & Beutell, N.J. (1987).

Sex differences in coping with career decision
making. <u>Journal</u> <u>of</u> <u>Vocational</u> <u>Behavior,</u> <u>31,</u>
174-181.

This report investigated sex differences in
coping with career decision making among 247
undergraduates. Men and women differed on
three of four coping factors. Men scored
significantly higher on Self-Efficacy Behavior
while women scored higher on Reactive Behavior
and Support Seeking Behavior. It was found
that the pattern of relationships between
coping and career indecision was virtually
identical for both sexes.

243.   Osipow, S.H. (1990). Convergence in
theories of career choice and development:
Review and prospect. <u>Journal</u> <u>of</u> <u>Vocational</u>
<u>Behavior,</u> <u>36,</u> 122-131.

Theories of career choice and development have
exerted an active force on vocational research
and counseling practice for more than 40
years. As the major theories have evolved,
the influence of some diminished, while those
remaining influential have come to resemble
each other in important ways. This paper
analyzes these similarities in order to
determine whether the field is moving toward
an integrated theory. The analysis leads to
the conclusion that commonality exists in many
major ways, but that some differences between
the theories remain and are useful for
specific populations and purposes.

244.   Pask-McCartney, C., & Salomone, P.R.
(1988). Different cases in career counseling:
III - The multipotential client. <u>Career</u>
<u>Development</u> <u>Quarterly,</u> <u>36,</u> 231-240.

This study discusses counseling methods for
individuals who, by virtue of their multiple
interests, talents, skills, and drives,
present unique career-making difficulties for

themselves. Advantages and disadvantages of
multipotentiality for career counseling are
considered. Method for identifying clients
whose multipotentiality interfere with career
decision making are offered as are practical
suggestions for the counseling processes.

245.   Plaud, J.J., Baker, R.W., & Groccia,
J.E. (1990). Freshmen decidedness regarding
academic major and anticipated and actual
adjustment to an engineering college. NACADA
Journal, 10, 20-26.

The relationship between freshmen decidedness
and actual adjustment to an engineering
college was investigated. Positive relation
was found between decidedness regarding
academic major and both anticipated adjustment
(measured prematriculation) and actual
adjustment (measured postmatriculation). The
relation was clearer postmatriculation than
prematriculation and was strongest for
academic adjustment and weakest for social
adjustment.

246.   Romer, L. (1985). Faculty
responsibility and college student career
decisions. College Student Journal, 17, 163-
165.

Assistance to college students making career
decisions about their lives after graduation
are usually left to placement offices or
counseling centers. This is seen to be not
sufficient because such organizations lack
adequate knowledge of the student's training,
of the opportunities and requirements of the
field into which the student wishes to go, and
of the student's capacities. Students would
be better served if faculty, through
major departments and in concert with
placement and counseling offices, advise about
graduate schools, employment opportunities in
the field, and the need for continuing

education.

247.   Roth,   M.J.   (1985).   The   LAUNCH
program: An   advising   tool.   Journal   of
College Placement, 45, 57-61.

The LAUNCH (Learning and Understanding - Not
Choosing Haphazardly) program is described.   A
series of questionnaires is provided to assist
advisers in helping students' thinking about
goals, skills, values, and careers.

248.   Sampson, J.P., Jr., et al. (1990).   A
differential feature   cost-analysis   of   nine
computer-assisted career   guidance   systems.
Journal of Career Development, 17, 81-111.

Nine computer-assisted career guidance systems
were assessed.   They   included   the   Career
Information System,   Choices,   Choices   for
Adults, Choices Jr., Discover, and Sigi-Plus.
Four detailed tables compare features in terms
of career   decision-making   content,   user
friendliness, support materials and services,
and costs.

249.   Swanson, J.L., & Tokar, D.M. (1991).
College students' perceptions of barriers to
career development.   Journal of Vocational
Behavior, 38, 92-106.

Students' perceptions   of   the   existence   of
career-related barriers   varied   across   six
categories: a) choice of major, b) getting
the degree or training, c) getting the first
job, d) advancing in a career, e) balancing
career and family, and f) special concerns of
women. The greatest impediments to choosing a
major and career were not being informed, not
being capable, current and future financial
concerns, and significant others' influence.
No significant differences were found for the
types of barriers listed by women and men.

250.   Wallace, G.R., & Walker, S.P. (1990).
Self-concept, vocational interests, and choice
of academic major in college students.
College Student Journal, 23, 361-367.

This study reported on the level of self-
concept and the degree of congruence between
college students' selection of an academic
major and their personality type or profile on
the Strong-Campbell Interest Inventory (SCII).
A multiple regression analysis confirmed the
research hypothesis that college students with
high self-concepts showed significantly more
congruence between their academic major and
vocational interest profiles than did students
with low self-concepts, and that the
relationship was not significantly affected by
gender and ethnic origin.

251.   Wilder, J.R. (1992). Academic and
career advising institutional commitment and
program recommendations. Peabody Journal of
Education, 59, 107-111.

It is the responsibility of the educational
institution to provide for the career-related
as well as the academic needs of its students.
These two basic concerns of institutions
wishing to implement a successful program of
academic and career advising focus on 14
recommended steps and funding requirements.

Chapter 7

Retention

252.   Backhus, D. (1989). Centralized intrusive advising and undergraduate retention. NACADA Journal, 9, 39-45.

This study sought to ascertain the influence of the Student Advising Center on retention. First year students entering in 1984 were compared to students who entered the university prior to the establishment of the advising center. The study discusses the impact of the centralized advising service which practices intrusive advising on the persistence of entering students and suggests that this strategy could be useful to other institutions.

253.   Beal, P.E., & Noel, L. (1980). What works in student retention. Iowa City, IA: American College Testing Program and the National Center for Higher Education Management Systems.

In this book retention research and action programs are reviewed and findings from a national survey on retention are examined. The survey was designed to identify, analyze, and compile information about campus efforts to improve student retention in higher

education. Three general areas of concern are
identified: 1) academic stimulations and
directions, 2) personal future building by
helping students to clarify their goals and
directions, and 3) involvement experiences
directed at students.

254.   Boyd, V. et al. (1990). Impact of a
career exploration component on student
retention: A replication. (Research Report
No. 6-90). College Park: University of
Maryland Counseling Center.

In this study, students enrolled in an
academic survival course that included a self-
help career exploration component, displayed a
higher retention rate than did students
enrolled in an academic survival course
without the self-help component. Four years
later, the results of a similar comparison
revealed that the students who had completed
the self-help career exploration component had
lower retention rates than did the other
students in the academic survival course.
Possible explanations for this are discussed.

255.   Brookman, D.M. (1989). Maslow's
hierarchy and student retention. NACADA
Journal, 9, 69-74.

Abraham Maslow's hierarchy of needs offers
perspectives on student motivation and a
rationale for college retention programming.
This article discusses how student affairs and
faculty interventions addressing student
safety needs and engaging students' sense of
purpose reinforce persistence. A mentor
program is a possible cooperative effort
between student personnel and teaching staff.

256.   Creamer, D.G. (1980). Educational
advising for student retention: An
institutional perspective. Community College
Review, 7, 11-18.

This article discusses how effective educational advising can have an impact on retention. This analysis of literature suggests seven propositions for consideration when organizing an advising program. Each of these propositions are discussed in the perspective of possible relevance for increasing student retention. The propositions are then generalized to formulate a model for advising for retention.

257.   Ethington, C.A. (1990). A psychological model of student persistence. Research in Higher Education, 31, 279-293.

This study examined the validity of the Eccles model of achievement behaviors (model of academic choice) for its predictive validity when the outcome (behavior) is student persistence to the completion of the baccalaureate degree. Of the two constructs hypothesized to directly influence persistence (the value placed on college attendance and expectations for success in college), only value had significant influence. Two measures of goal orientation, business/financial and humanitarian/social, exerted indirect influences as hypothesized, but level of degree aspiration had as strong direct influence on persistences as did value. Prior achievement had the strongest total effect of any of the variables in the model.

258.   Fuller, A.G. (1983). A strategy to improve retention. NACADA Journal, 3, 65-72.

A freshman counseling program consisting of academic, career, and personal counseling and study skills, separate from departmental advising, was implemented in an effort to improve student retention. This goal was accomplished with no sacrifice in student academic standing and with favorable student response. The program and its accomplishments are discussed.

259.   Glennen, R.E., & Bexley, D.M. (1985).
Reduction of attrition through intrusive
advising. NASPA Journal, 22, 10-14.
An intrusive advising program is outlined that
successfully reduced attrition of high-risk
college freshmen and sophomores. The program
was based on the philosophy that the
university should call students in for
advising numerous times during the year
instead of the normal once-a-semester meeting.
Ten faculty members were assigned to the
General College on released time. The faculty
advisers received training prior to the
beginning of each fall semester. Freshmen
attrition was reduced from 66 percent to 48
percent the first year and from 48 percent to
25 percent the second year.

260.   Goldman, B.A. (1988). It's time to
provide higher education courses in enrollment
management, academic advising, and retention.
College Student Journal, 22, 42-46.

Enrollment management, academic advising, and
retention are key factors on American college
campuses. All three are of vital concern to
higher education as they have direct impact
upon retention. This article discusses the
inception of these activities, the personnel
to direct them, and the extensive interaction
that these activities generate within the
total campus community. Given the recent
attention directed toward enrollment,
advising, and retention and the paucity of
instruction offered by higher education
graduate programs in these areas, the author
urges the inclusion of such instruction in
higher education graduate programs.
Descriptions of courses offered by the author
in these areas are presented for
consideration.

261. Habley, W.R. (1981). Academic advisement: The critical link in student retention. NASPA Journal, 18, 45-50.

This paper looks at direct and critical elements in retention strategy between academic advisement and retention using a proposed Advisement-Retention Model. The model is predicated on two assumptions: 1) quality academic advising should be student-centered and a developmental process, not prescriptive and clerical; 2) although an institution can effectively orchestrate those variables which lead to retention, an institution may not be able to reverse effectively all the variables which lead to attrition. Application of the model brings the contribution to the staying environment by assisting the student in exploring individual goals and integrating those goals into academic offerings, in identifying relevant classwork, and in course selection appropriate to student capabilities.

262. Jackson, C. (1978). Academic advising and student attrition. (ERIC Document Reproduction Service No. ED 165 550)

The relationship between academic advising and student attrition is examined through a cohort analysis of students entering a small liberal arts college over a four year period in which advising was done by faculty. Results indicate that there is a wide distribution of withdrawn students according to initial faculty adviser (no indications that specific advisers have disproportionate withdrawals) and that there is a relationship between faculty experience and student withdrawal.

263. Janasiewicz, B.A. (1987). Campus leaving behavior. NACADA Journal, 7, 23-30.

This study sought to identify reasons for

students' leaving behavior. Three distinct
models of leaving behavior were identified
from the results: Discouraged Student Model,
an Academic Model, and a Financial Model.
Implications for academic advising are
discussed.

264.   Kapraun, E.D., Jr., & Coldren, D.W.
(1982). Academic advising to facilitate
student retention. NACADA Journal, 2, 59-69.

This article describes how academic advising
can facilitate student retention by examining
seven components of an advising program.
These seven components are: institutional
commitment to academic advising, faculty-
endorsed statement of adviser responsibilities
with retention as a major component, training
advisers, adviser evaluation and recognition,
peer advisers to assist faculty advisers,
well-defined referral system, and existence of
an information support system. Following
discussion of these seven components, the
authors suggest two caveats: advising is not a
cure-all but one of eight dimensions of
retention programs, and, it takes two to five
years to implement a comprehensive retention
program.

265.   King, M.C. (1993). Academic
advising, retention, and transfer. In M.C.
King (Ed.) Academic advising: organizing and
delivering services for student success. New
Directions for Community Colleges, No. 82.
San Francisco: Jossey-Bass.

This chapter discusses the importance of
academic advising in student retention and
transfer. A summary of Tinto's model of
student departure is followed by a review of
some of the research that operationalizes that
model. Themes of attrition and the role that
advisers play are described. The chapter
concludes with a discussion of the importance

of the transfer function and the role of
advisers in enhancing transfer.

266.   Kinlock, G.C., Frost, G.A., & MacKay,
C. (1993). Academic dismissal, readmission
conditions, and retention: A study of social
science majors. NACADA Journal, 13, 18-22.

This study focused on approximately 500 social
science majors who were dismissed from a large
state university. In addition to background
and academic traits, specific conditions of
their readmission on academic success and
retention were also studied. At this
university the data indicated that at-risk
social science students tend more often to be
Whites, African-Americans, Hispanics, males,
juniors, transfer students, those in their mid
20's, those with interdisciplinary and
limited-access majors, and those with low high
school GPA's. Academic success among those
who were readmitted was significantly
associated with gender, quality point deficit,
and certain readmission conditions. The
authors suggest important advising/counseling
considerations from the trends identified in
this study.

267.   Kramer, G.L., Moss, R.D., Taylor,
L.T., & Hendrix, L.J. (1985). Why students
persist in college: A categorical analysis.
NACADA Journal, 5, 1-17.

Generally, according to the authors, retention
research exists in two forms. The study is
designed to measure the effectiveness of
retention programs, or it seeks to establish
cause and effect relationships between one or
several variables and attrition. This study
presents the results of research which
concentrated on the latter. It also sought to
determine the differences between "persisters"
and "leavers" in relation to their goals of
attending college, and the effects of social

and academic integration associated with
institutional commitment. Subpopulations and
former nongraduated students were studied.
Implications for research are offered.

268.   Levin, J., & Wyckoff, J. (1988).
Effective advising: Identifying students most
likely to persist and succeed in engineering.
Engineering Education, 78, 178-182.

Over 1,000 freshmen engineering students
participated in a pre-enrollment testing,
counseling, and advising program. Admissions
records and transcript information from the
completed freshman year were obtained.
Logistic regression analyses revealed that
anticipated study time per week and gender
were strongly predictive of cumulative GPA.
Two other nonintellective variables also
contributed to the prediction: nonscience
points, and reason for choosing engineering.

269.   Lopez, M., Yanez, M., Clayton, E.R.,
& Thompson, D.A. (1988). Intrusive advising
with special student populations. NASPA
Journal, 25, 195-201.

This article describes the use of an intrusive
advising program with a number of special
student populations, including educationally
disadvantaged students admitted through an
alternative admissions program, minority
students, learning disabled students, and
severely economically disadvantaged migrant
students. Retention implications are covered.

270.   Miller, M.B. (1985). A positive
approach to student retention: The academic
advising, intervention and monitoring system.
NACADA Journal, 5, 19-24.

When a community college faced an eleven
percent drop in enrollment, advising and other
interventions were examined as factors in

reversing the decline. Strategies that successfully reversed the drop in enrollment are described. These included faculty and staff involvement and a creative problem-solving approach.

271.   Noel, L., Levitz, R., Saluri, D., & Associates. (1985). Increasing student retention. San Francisco: Jossey-Bass.

This action-oriented book contains examples of successful retention programs. The first part presents a comprehensive overview of the concepts and principles involved in student attrition and retention. These include chapters on understanding who stays, who leaves, and what makes the difference. The second and third parts offer guidelines for practitioners interested in improving the quality of retention programs, services and activities on their campuses. These include targeting specific groups of students who are at risk for dropping out such as low income, underprepared, undecided, adult and commuter students. The final part describes processes for creating campus wide change efforts for improving the quality of retention programs and services for students. These include assessment approaches, increasing faculty involvement and case studies of successful programs.

272.   Patrick, J., Furlow, J.W., & Donovan, S. (1988). Using a comprehensive academic intervention program in the retention of high-risk students. NACADA Journal, 8, 29-34.

The use of a comprehensive academic advising program in conjunction with a sustained academic orientation program through the freshman year has resulted in a 13 percent increase in the retention rate of high-risk students at a regional campus of a large public research university. In this article, the authors describe the components of CORE, the comprehensive advising/orientation program, and the success they've had with high-risk students in the program.

273.   Shaney, M.O., & Witten, C.H. (1990). U101 freshman seminar course: A longitudinal study of persistence, retention and graduation rates. NASPA Journal, 27, 344-352.

This study involved an elective, one-semester pass-fail course for freshmen to acquaint them in small groups with the goals of higher education and the university and its support programs, services and extracurricular activities. Data were obtained on persistence over three years and graduation seven years after entry. Scores revealed that participants had higher rates of graduation for each of the first three years, proportionately more of the participants than of the nonparticipants, and persistence rates after seven years were higher for both white and African-American participants than for their nonparticipant counterparts.

274.   Spanard, J.M.A. (1990). Beyond intent: Reentering college to complete the degree. Review of Educational Research, 60, 309-344.

A descriptive model is proposed to describe the path of adult problem solving and thinking that leads to reentry into college, retention, and eventual completion of a college degree. Intrinsic and extrinsic facilitators and inhibitors to degree completion, theories of motivation, and persistence are explore in this article.

275.   Swift, J.S. (1987). Retention of adult college students. NACADA Journal, 7, 7-19.

There are many studies dealing with retention
of traditional college-age students, but few
about retention of adult students. What is
lacking is data about adults who do not finish
a degree program, and data that indicate
whether or not adults follow the patterns that
characterize traditional college-age students.
In this article some of the reasons
traditional college-age students withdraw are
applied to adults, as summarized by a review
of the literature. In addition to offering
additional conclusions regarding adults who
persist versus those who drop out, suggestions
are given for increasing the retention of
adult learners.

276.   Tinto, V. (1987). Leaving college.
Chicago: University of Chicago Press.

The first part of this book provides an
overview of the extensive body of research on
student attrition and proposes a theory to
give it order. The theory provides a view of
student leaving and institutional action which
stresses the limits and responsibility of an
institution's share in the education of its
students. The book also offers suggestions
for increasing student retention in higher
education. It outlines discrete steps and
proposes a course of action that can be
applied to many settings. Chapters in the
book highlight the dimensions of student
leaving, the scope of patterns of departure,
and the roots of individual departure.
Suggestions for institutional action are also
given.

277.   Tinto, V. (1988). Stages of student
departure: Reflections on the longitudinal
character of student leaving.
Journal of Higher Education, 59, 438-455.

Expanding upon existing literature, it is
argued that the longitudinal process of

student departure, far from being uniform
across time, is marked by distinct stages
which reflect the unique problems individuals
encounter in seeking to become incorporated
into the life the institution. Research and
policy implications are discussed.

Chapter 8

Legal Issues in Advising

278.   Am I liable? Faculty, staff and
institutional liability in the college and
university settings. (1989). Washington,
D.C.: National Association of College and
University Attorneys.

This book examines issues related to college
and university liability. Chapter one
provides an introduction and overview of tort
law concepts, defining them in terms of
college and university liabilities. The next
two chapters focus on the criminal acts of
third persons. Chapters four and five address
current liability issues related to academic
advising, peer review, letters of
recommendation, and workers' compensation
laws. Chapter six discusses liability release
and forms for college and university
extracurricular activities. A structural
overview for analyzing risk management and
insurance procurement is provided in the final
chapter.

279.   Barr, M.J. (1988). Student services
and the law: A handbook for practitioners.
San Francisco: Jossey-Bass.

This sourcebook contains 19 chapters on

providing a legally defensible student affairs
environment. Part one covers the legal
foundations of student affairs. Key areas of
legal responsibilities and liability are
examined in part two. Part three covers
specific policies and procedures to strengthen
the legal basis of an institution's diverse
student services and correctly applies various
legal sources. Topics covered include
admissions, counseling and health services,
student discipline, student records, and the
supervision of staff members. The book
concludes with an outline of emerging legal
themes expected to affect student affairs.

280.   Davenport, D. (1985).   The catalog in
the courtroom: From shield to sword? Journal
of College and University Law, 12, 201-226.

Legal issues concerning the content and use of
the college catalog are reviewed, including
the catalog's changing role as a consumer
document, misrepresentation, violation of
statute, breach of contract, court
interpretations, and remedies. Colleges are
cautioned to take great care in using catalogs
for legal and administrative reasons.

281.   Drowatzky, J.N. (1991). Legal issues
regarding curriculum: What administrators
need to know about curriculum and its
delivery. (ERIC Document Reproduction Service
No. ED 331 454)

This paper focuses upon a variety of
curriculum related issues that have potential
legal connotations, such as whether the
college bulletin forms a contract, whether
advertisements can be considered contracts,
and determining the appropriateness of student
discipline for academic and other reasons. A
brief overview of contract law is given as
well as an explanation of express contracts.
Other topics include implied promise or quasi-

contract, discipline and expulsion, and
educational malpractice. Courts have seen the
administration of educational programs and
activities as belonging in the hands of the
educators so long as there is no abuse of
educational rules and regulations. Students
must be able to meet all the requirements of
the programs they wish to enter, however,
including both academic and non-academic
requirements.

282.   Gehring, D.D. (1984). Legal issues
in academic advising. In R. Winston, T.
Miller, S. Ender, and T. Grites (Eds.)
Developmental academic advising. San
Francisco: Jossey-Bass.

This chapter provides an introduction to the
primary legal relationships that impinge upon
the advising process and the rights and
responsibilities of the parties involved in
those relationships. The advising process
involves constitutional parameters,
contractual obligations, statutory mandates,
and the rights of the students to be free from
damage to their persons, property, or
reputations. Each of these relationships is
discussed in the context of educational
advising. Academic advisers who understand
these relationships will be better able to
detect the legal issues that arise every day
in the advising process.

283.   Gehring, D.D. (1987). The legal
limitations on statements made by advisers.
NACADA Journal, 7 64-68.

This article reviews the role of the academic
adviser as an "agent" entitling the adviser to
specific legal privilege but also holding the
adviser accountable for actions taken within
the scope of his or her employment. Acting
beyond this scope could be grounds for
personal liability rather than liability as an

agent of the college or university. This
article outlines the legal parameters that
define the liability of an adviser for
statements made in transmitting information to
or about students.

284.   Miles, A.S., & Seymour, J.C. (1986).
The contractual relationship between students
and the university. College Student Affairs
Journal, 7, 7-15.

Breach of contract is one of the main causes
of actions students use to sue an institution
of higher education. Contracts between
students and their institution can take the
form of admissions agreements, housing
contracts, student handbooks, or oral
statements made by a school representative.
Three remedies may be applied against the
breaching person or institution: monetary
damages, injunction, and/or direction of
specific performance. This article discusses
a number of steps that colleges and
universities can take to safeguard against
problems with contractual relationships with
students.

285.   Miller, T.K., & Winston, R.B. (Eds.)
(1991). Administration and leadership in
student affairs: Actualizing student
development in higher education (2nd ed.).
Muncie, IN: Accelerated Development. (ERIC
Document Reproduction Service No. ED 344 144)

This book addresses both theoretical and
practical issues faced by entry-level and mid-
level practitioners who espouse a commitment
to student development. Among the twenty-
three chapters are topics covering ethical
professional practice, standards of
professional practice, legal issues in
administration, and an introduction to legal
research.

286.   Mosier, G.C. (1989).   Why students
sue.   AGB Reports, 31, 27-29.

Student lawsuits challenging an institution's
academic standards and grades are usually of
three types: challenging grades as arbitrary
and subjective, allegations of noncompliance
with right to due process, and accusations of
misconduct that a student feels are false and
defamatory.   Matters of academic misconduct
are more closely scrutinized by the courts,
especially cases involving a student's right
to due process.   Policies that can help to
limit liability include the formulation of a
fair appeal's process, the establishment of
clear grading criteria by faculty members, and
policies that ensure that academic matters are
left as much as possible to faculty members.

287.   Nowicki, M. (1987).   Legal
implications of academic advising.   NACADA
Journal, 7, 83-86.

This article examines some of the basic legal
relationships and basic tort law in connection
with academic advising.   The contractual
relationship between the student and the
institution, the constitutional relationship,
statutory relationship, and tort law are
examined.   This article is offered primarily
for the benefit of new academic advisers, and
it can also serve as a quick review for
experienced advisers.

288.   Owens, H.F. (1980). They'll take you
to court if you don't watch out.   Community
and Junior College Journal, 51, 12-16.

This article describes several bases of
litigation brought by students against
instructors.   One of the areas explained is
proper instruction.   College officials are
cautioned to accurately deliver what is put
forth in both written and oral statements.

Another obligation that has been upheld by the courts for instructors is adequate supervision of both in- and out-of-class activities that are instructionally related. Tort liability could arise when an instructor fails to supervise or supervises improperly. Faculty members are encouraged to take their advising responsibilities as seriously as class instruction responsibilities. Suggestions for the avoidance of tort liability in these areas are made.

289.   Schubert, A.F., & Schubert, G.W. (1983). Academic advising and potential litigation. NACADA Journal, 3, 1-11.

The academic adviser is vulnerable. Due to the responsibilities and duties placed upon the academic adviser, legal actions may result. In this article, issues in tort and contract law and recent experiences in litigation that influence the academic adviser's responsibility are outlined. Included in these are negligence, nondisclosure, misrepresentation, defamation, written and oral contracts, and the adviser as an agent of the institution. Specific areas of adviser vulnerability are noted.

290.   Schubert, A.F., & Schubert, G.W. (1986). The student-athlete: Ethical and legal issues. NACADA Journal, 6, 53-66.

The problem of corrupting the integrity of athletes and athletic programs is spreading because of the degree of competitive activities of the major sports. Leaders and rule makers have attempted to establish rules and regulations that clearly define the boundaries of the NCAA, and establish controls that are functional.

291.   Young, D.P. (1982). Legal issues regarding academic advising. NACADA Journal,

2, 41-45.

The increased number of decisions dealing with
classroom and academic matters attests to the
growing judicial sensitivity to student's
rights in academic affairs. The adviser's job
falls within this academic affairs area, and
thus, advisers must understand the legal
issues involving four major areas: the
contractual relationship between student and
institution, guidelines governing privacy of
student records, the concept of privileged
communications, and academic due process and
the need for grievance procedures.

292.   Young, D.P. (1984).   Legal issues
regarding academic advising: An update.
NACADA Journal, 4, 89-85.

The author suggests that if academicians do
not abuse their discretion in dealing with
students, they need not fear judicial
intervention. The courts will intervene,
however, if evidence exists of arbitrary or
negligent treatment of students or denial of
their protected rights. Academic advisers
must understand the legal issues involving
such areas as the contractual relationship
between student and institution, the statutory
relationship, the guidelines governing privacy
of student records, the concept of privileged
communications, the academic due process, and
the need for grievance procedures.

Chapter 9

Advising As A Profession

293.   Bee, R.H., Beronja, T.A., & Mann, G. (1990). Analysis of the unionization of academic advisers. NACADA Journal, 10, 35-40.

Professional/administrative personnel at colleges and universities must address not only the challenges to student populations, but also their own professional and personal needs. The relatively small number in this "middle-management" group (e.g., academic advising, career counseling, admissions counseling) has been a hindrance to its collective strength in obtaining economic, career and professional goals. The professional/administrative staff at Youngstown State University pursued an innovative course, unionization, in an attempt to achieve these desired goals. The question examined is whether unionization produced the outcomes these professionals had envisioned it would.

294.   Goetz, J.J., & White, E.R. (1986). A survey of graduate programs addressing the preparation of professional academic advisers. NACADA Journal, 6, 43-47.

This study investigated the extent to which

graduate programs in higher education and
college student personnel offer their students
courses and/or practical experiences to
prepare for positions as professional academic
advisers. The article raises the following
questions: 1) Should professional staff
academic advisers positions be considered
similar to faculty positions; that is, should
advisers perform within and be evaluated on
the traditional faculty model of teaching,
research and service within tenure and
promotion structure? 2) Should professional
staff academic advising positions be
considered similar to student services
positions; that is, should advisers perform
and be evaluated on the traditional student
affairs model of service to students? or 3)
Does the nature of academic advising in the
university allow for a reformation of the
traditional faculty and student services
models toward a "hybrid" model for
professional staff academic advising
positions?

295.   Gordon, V.N. (1982). Training future
academic advisers: One model of a pre-service
approach. NACADA Journal, 2, 35-40.

This is a description of a graduate-level
course that is designed to prepare future
professional academic advisers while they are
enrolled in their graduate training. This
pre-service approach provides an understanding
of advising as a process and a professional
activity. The course, taught at The Ohio
State University, is described in terms of
course objectives, content, requirements,
materials, and evaluation procedures. A model
syllabus is provided. The author encourages
graduate programs in higher education and
related areas to provide courses in academic
advising so future faculty and professional
advisers may receive training in its purpose
and functions before entering the job market.

296.   Gordon, V.N., et al. (1988).
Advising as a profession. <u>NACADA Journal,</u> <u>8,</u>
59-64.

This article summarizes a study to provide a
general picture of advising nationally. The
survey solicited ideas and opinions of
academic advising as a profession. A
questionnaire was mailed to the entire
membership at the time; there was a 72%
response. The survey revealed no patterns or
obvious similarities in advising systems, in
titles, or in contractual rights and salaries.
It was found that 50% of the respondents
advised part-time while carrying out other
duties such as teaching or orientation. Many
other issues concerning advising as a
profession are discussed.

297.   Gordon, V.N. (1992). Advising as a
profession. In V. Gordon, <u>Handbook</u> <u>of</u>
<u>academic</u> <u>advising.</u> Westport, CT: Greenwood
Press.

This chapter examines many issues involved in
advising as a profession. First, definitions
of a "profession" are researched and how
academic advising relates to those definitions
is discussed. The role of professional
advisers is compared to that of faculty
advisers. Job descriptions, preparation,
mobility, salaries, unionization, and
performance appraisal are discussed. Ethical
behavior and legal issues are also discussed
in the context of professional advisers'
responsibilities to students and the
institution.

298.   Habley, W.R. (1986). Show us the
future: The challenges facing academic
advising. <u>NACADA</u> <u>Journal,</u> <u>6,</u> 5-11.

In order to improve the current low status of
academic advising, the author states that the

profession must confront the following eight
challenges: 1) developing a body of research,
2) providing evidence of specific and positive
outcomes, 3) enlisting the support of campus
decision-makers, 4) protecting advising
programs during times of budget cutbacks, 5)
elevating the status of advising by faculty
members, 6) using technology in support of
advising programs, 7) advancing academic
advising as a profession by setting standards,
and 8) creating career paths for academic
advising professionals.

299.   Kramer, H.C. (1984).   Academic
advising: Images of a profession.   (ERIC
Document Reproduction Service No. ED 249 826)

In this document, the level of professional
development and functioning of academic
advising is discussed.   A three-level scheme
is used to assess the level of professional
development.   When the offerings at the
National Conference on Academic Advising were
studied, 46 percent were intended for an
audience functioning at level one, which means
primarily identified to their professional
subspecialty and subunit.   Thirty-nine percent
were designed for level two, which are those
whose primary identification is to the entire
student enterprise.   Finally, 15 percent of
the presentations were directed toward the
interests of level three, which are those who
are most effectively conceptually linked with
others, because their programs are interwoven
with the bulk of the institution's goals that
extend beyond the realm of support services.

300.   Kramer, H.C. (1986).   Faculty
development: The advising coordinator's
changing scene.   NACADA Journal, 6, 31-42.

Faculty development is now shifting from the
margins of institutions to the center.   The
author recognizes that if institutions of

higher education are to remain dynamic and
alive, capable of growing qualitatively in an
increasingly restricted market, advising
coordinators must attend to faculty vitality.
In this context, institutional vitality will
require imaginative linking of professional
development of individual faculty with
carefully planned development of academic
programs and institutional policies.   463.

301.   Lowenstein, M., & Grites, T.J.
(1993). Ethics in academic advising. <u>NACADA</u>
<u>Journal, 13,</u> 53-61.

Academic advisors confront many ethical
problems and benefit from being able to draw
on a system of ethical principles. Such
principles, to be credible, should be
philosophically defensible and not merely
reflective of individual tastes. This article
proposes such a set of principles, shows how
they can be used to cope with ethical
dilemmas, and explains why such dilemmas
cannot be prevented. These principles are
intended to be useful in training academic
advisers but are not intended to create a code
of ethics for advising.

302.   McMillian, M., & Ivy, W.A. (1990).
The role of professional academic advisers in
curriculum development grants. <u>NACADA</u>
<u>Journal, 10,</u> 30-34.

Academic advising can make important
contributions in implementing curriculum
development grants received by
universities. This article presents, in case
study form, an advising and orientation plan
developed for a National Science Foundation
grant to prepare future science and math
teachers. This plan discusses comprehensive
recruitment strategies, a specially designed
orientation course, off-campus retreats and
field experiences, and academic advising and

career counseling. The plan fostered a sense
of community among faculty and students as
well as a commitment to the program.   This
contributed to the success of the project and
could contribute to similar grants as well.

303.   Midgen, J. (1989).   The professional
adviser.   NACADA Journal, 9, 63-68.

The purpose of this article is to create among
higher education administrators an awareness
of the importance of developing and
implementing an advising system that can
satisfy most of the needs of its students.
The author discusses the value of professional
advisers in an overall advising program.
Comparisons are made among faculty, peer, and
professional advisers, discussing the
contributions of each type.   Evidence and some
observations are presented to support the
contention that this objective is more likely
to be achieved when professional advisers are
recognized as an integral part, along with
faculty and peer advisors, of the advising
process.

304.   Olson, C.M. (1981).   Professional
academic advising and career planning: An
integrated approach.   Journal of College
Student Personnel, 22, 483-488.

This article presents a case study in which
one university sociology department integrated
advising, curriculum planning, and career
guidance. The objectives of this article are
to: 1) support an argument for a synthesis of
academic advising and career guidance, 2)
argue that a non-faculty professional academic
counselor can implement and continue this
process more efficiently and effectively than
faculty, 3) argue that the professional
academic adviser can act effectively as a
facilitator of communication, a coordinator of
learning experiences, and a referral agent.

305.   Wrenn, C.G., & Darley, J.G. (1949).
An appraisal of the professional status of
personnel work. In E.G. Williamson (Ed.)
Trends in student personnel work.
Minneapolis: The University of Minnesota
Press.

Discussing the professional status of
personnel work, the article covers the
following topics: 1) the application of
standards, selection, and training, 2) the
definition of job titles and function, 3) the
possession of specialized knowledge and
skills, 4) the development of a professional
consciousness and professional groups, 5) the
self-imposition of standards of admission and
performance, 6) legal recognition of the
vocation, 7) the development of a code of
ethics, and 8) the performance of a socially
needed function. The authors believe that the
trend toward professionalization has improved
the standards of personnel services and
permitted these services to discharge better
the responsibilities to students and to other
personnel professionals.

306.   Young, R.B. (1988).   The
profession(ization) of student affairs.
(1988).   NASPA Journal, 25, 262-266.

This article promotes the view of student
affairs as dynamic and professionalizing
rather than static and professionalized.
Professionalization is a concept which must be
applied to all occupations in a world of
change. Status is not an end in itself; it is
earned by the good work of practitioners.
Growing must be the fundamental characteristic
of the field.

Chapter 10

Evaluation and Assessment

307.   Alexander, J.M., & Stark, J.S. (1986). <u>Focusing on student academic outcomes. A working paper.</u> Ann Arbor, MI: National Center for Research to Improve Postsecondary Teaching and Learning. (ERIC Document Reproduction Service No. ED 287 431)

Current methods and instruments for assessing college student outcomes are identified and described, and possible outcome measures are suggested. College outcomes are defined from several perspectives. Various approaches to outcome assessment as well existing typologies are included. Several outcome measures are discussed including academic-cognitive outcomes, academic-motivational, and academic-behavorial. Charts and references are included.

308.   Allard, S. (1992). <u>BBCC transfer student follow-up: Washington State University students reflect upon Big Bend Community College education.</u> Moses Lake, WA: Big Bend Community College Office of Assessment. (ERIC Document Reproduction Service No. ED 344 637)

A team of Big Bend Community College faculty members traveled to Washington State

University to survey and interview former BBCC
students enrolled at WSU. The purpose of the
investigation was to assess the effectiveness
of BBCC in preparing students for transfer to
and continued success at the four-year college
level, and to measure BBCC's effect on the
students' abilities and skills. Each student
met with the team and completed a short
evaluative survey. Following the survey, each
student participated in an interview
discussion with at least one faculty member
focusing on issues of educational quality and
improvement at BBCC. An area identified as a
weakness was academic/curriculum advising and
students offered specific recommendations for
improvement. Data tables, verbatim student
comments, and the survey instruments are
included.

309.   Aquino, F.J. (1990, May). A typology
of community college student behaviors:
Defining student success and student failure.
AIR 1990 Annual Forum Paper. Paper presented
at the Annual Forum of the Association for
Institutional Research, Louisville, KY. (ERIC
Document Reproduction Service No. ED 321 678).

A model is presented for creating a community
college student typology for the purpose of
defining successful and unsuccessful student
outcomes for each typology segment. The need
for such a typology is addressed, as well as a
description given of the computer techniques
used to gather the baseline data upon which
the typology is based, and the methodology
used to generate the typology. The major
portion of the study deals with the typology
itself and the success criteria defined for
each student type along with actual
achievement percentages; these percentages are
compared to the established goals assigned for
each type. The typology was constructed out
of two key variables: initial course load and
stated intention.

310.   Astin, A.W. (1991). Assessment for
excellence: The philosophy and practice of
assessment and evaluation in higher education.
New York: American Council on Education and
Macmillan.

This book presents a detailed critique of
traditional assessment policies and addresses
the major issues related to assessment. It
reviews different approaches to assessment
including value-added testing, incentive
funding, competency testing and challenge
grants. A detailed model (the I-E-O design)
forms the basis for the book. Also included
are the theory and conceptualization of
assessment and evaluation, the statistical
techniques for analyzing assessment data, and
the practical problems of
disseminating assessment results to various
audiences.

311.   Balenger, V.J., Sedlacek, W.E., &
Osteen, J.M. (1989). Prescriptive evaluation
plans: A method of large-scale evaluation in
student affairs (Research Report #16-19).
(ERIC Document Reproduction Service No. ED 312
310)

A method for evaluation that is appropriate
for a student affairs department that contains
more than one service unit is described. A
staff member in each service unit is appointed
to conduct that unit's self-study, with the
consultative help of an experienced evaluation
coordinator. For each unit, the evaluation
coordinator develops a Prescriptive Evaluation
Plan (PEP) to guide the self-study. The
article discusses the different criteria for
the plans.

312.   Banta, T. (1991). Linking outcomes
assessment and the freshman experience.
Journal of the Freshman Year Experience, 3,
93-108.

A review of externally mandated outcomes
assessment activities and resulting
innovations in freshman programs focuses on
efforts in Tennessee and Virginia, in which
higher education funding is linked to outcomes
assessment. Areas examined include
registration, advising, student-faculty
contact, computer use, basic skills, staff
development, student-student contact, and
curriculum.

313.   Barger, R.N., & Barger, J.C. (1981).
The two edges of advisement: Report of a
national survey. (ERIC Document Reproduction
Service No. ED 210 989)

The state of academic advisement in postsecondary education was studied through a
survey of representatives of 58 colleges and
universities and students who were pursuing
undergraduate degrees in four year
institutions during the 1960's, 1970's, and
1980's. For the three time periods, there was
marked decrease in public school student
satisfaction with their advisement and a
corresponding increase in private school
student satisfaction. Students viewed
themselves as the most helpful resource in
making decisions about majors, teachers as the
most helpful external resource, and advisers
tied with friends as being least helpful. A
bibliography, sample questionnaires, and
sample student descriptions of an ideal
student advisement program are appended.

314.   Bers, T.H. (1992). The costs and
benefits of student tracking systems.
Community, Technical, and Junior College
Journal, 62, 20-23.

This article discusses student tracking system
development in terms of purposes, audience,
organizational issues, and data utilization.
Benefits include facilitating reporting

behavioral outcomes and illuminating the
complementary/conflicting nature of college
services. Direct costs for computer
programming, postage, printing, etc. are also
considered a benefit.

315.   Braxton, J.M. (1988). Casual
modeling and path analysis: An introduction
and an illustration in student attrition
research. Journal of College Student
Development, 29, 263-272.

This article describes path analysis as an
optimum data-analytic technique for research,
development, and evaluation of planned
interventions. It describes and illustrates
path analysis technique used in assessing the
influence of academic advising in student
persistence. The findings of this study
indicated that academic advising is two steps
removed from student persistence as its effect
is mediated by both academic integration and
subsequent institutional commitment. The
difficult task in the application of path
analysis is the development of causal models
that are consonant with sound theory or
substantive reasoning.

316.   Cavender, D.H. (1990). Improving the
effectiveness of advisory services through
performance appraisal. NACADA Journal, 10,
26-29.

In an attempt to increase the quality and
effectiveness of academic advising, a task
force at Auburn University examined the duties
and responsibilities of academic advisers.
From this job analysis, the author suggests a
behavioral results-oriented appraisal system
that can be used to assess the performance of
academic advisers.

317.   Cremer, C.V., & Ryan, M. (1984). New
techniques let students evaluate academic

advising. Journalism Educator, 39, 21-22.

This article describes a questionnaire that
was developed to measure student perceptions
of the quality of academic advising.
Completed questionnaires were analyzed and a
summary was presented to all faculty members.
Results of the study are discussed.

318.   Ford, J. (1985). Utilizing the
adviser perception inventory. NACADA Journal,
5, 63-68.

In order to help assess the effectiveness of
an academic advising system, an "Advisor
Perception Inventory" was used to add
information to the computer data bank. The
two summary reports generated from the
evaluation are discussed.

319.   Frisz, R.H., & Lane, J.R. (1987).
Student user evaluations of peer advising
services. Journal of College Student
Personnel, 28, 241-245.

In this study, the authors evaluate the
effectiveness of a peer advising program
through a questionnaire completed by students
who used the peer advising services. The
primary purposes of the peer advising program
were to provide general college information,
to discuss college adjustment, to help
students with a program of study, and to
explore career choices. Other aspects of the
program as well as the survey results are
discussed.

320.   Gardner, J., et al. (1990).
Guidelines for evaluating the freshman year
experience. Columbia, SC: Center for the
Study of the Freshman Year Experience. (ERIC
Document Reproduction Service No. ED 334 885)

This booklet presents questions that can be

used by a college or university task force
looking at the freshman year experience and/or
the broader undergraduate experience. It can
also be used to aid the process of campus
self-study or assessment. The questions are
arranged under three major headings: 1)
Campus Policies, Processes, and Climate; 2)
Academics; and 3) Student Life and Campus
Services. Questions are presented under the
following subheadings: recruitment/admissions;
orientation; institutional research and
resources; development of common culture and
community; institutional policies and goals
for the freshman year; the formal curriculum;
faculty and staff development; academic
advising and tutorial assistance; residence
life; student activities and campus services;
and campus problems and issues.

321.   Gordon, V.N. (1992). Evaluation.   In
V. Gordon, Handbook of Academic Advising.
Westport, CT: Greenwood Press.

This chapter summarizes many models of
evaluation including systematic, goal-
directed, and student-centered approaches.
The CAS Standards are described and their use
as a guide when creating an evaluation plan is
detailed. Evaluative methods are described
including surveys, questionnaires, computer
generated, and interview techniques. Other
factors included in this overall view of
evaluation in academic advising are
administrative support, involvement of
advisers, establishing program goals, setting
criteria, gathering and analyzing data, and
using the information for improving advising
services.

322.   Gordon, V.N., & Gardner, W. (1993).
computerized evaluation of academic advisers.
Journal of College Student Development, 34,
383-384.

This article describes an automated, computerized evaluation system that was developed for students to evaluate their academic adviser. The computer program was placed in strategic places in the advising center and students were encouraged to spend about four minutes to complete 15 items on the screen. The results were distributed to individual advisers and their immediate supervisors. The advantage of the computer program is that it is anonymous and students act as the data entry person as well as the respondee.

323.   Guinn, D., & Mitchell, R. (1986). Academic advising: And different expectations. NACADA Journal, 6, 99-105.

An Advising Role and Responsibility Inventory was developed and administered to test the hypothesis that differing perceptions of the role and responsibilities of the adviser exist. The population of the study consisted of students, faculty, and administrators from a four-year comprehensive, state-supported, midwestern university. The solution to the adviser's dilemma can be achieved only when all member of the advising educational family come to a consensus of what the adviser's role should be.

324.   Hanson, G.R., & Raney, M.W. (1993). Evaluating academic advising in a multiversity setting. NACADA Journal, 13, 34-42.

The purpose of this study was to evaluate the advising system at a complex multiversity and provide answers to both summative and formative evaluation questions. The results suggest that most students are advised, feel their advising needs have been met, and are satisfied with the help they receive. Students, in general, are less satisfied with the help they receive with specific issues and concerns. However, the results also show that relatively few students consider faculty to be their primary advisers, many students seek advising help from multiple sources, and a majority of students spend 15 minutes or less per semester with their primary adviser. Implications of these results for academic advising at multiversities are discussed.

325.   Iaccino, J.F. (1991). Assessment and comparison of advising for freshmen and upperclassmen. Journal of the Freshman Year Experience, 3, 75-90.

This study describes an evaluation of an advising program and seeks to compare satisfaction with advising among freshmen and upperclassmen. A locally developed instrument measured availability and accessibility, knowledge of major and graduation requirements. The results confirm the multi-faceted roles required of an adviser. Although providing accurate academic information was seen as important by students, a more personalized relationship was also emphasized.

326.   Jefcoat, H.G. (1991, October). Advisement intervention: A key strategy for a new age - student consumerism. Paper presented at the annual Convention of the National Rural Education Association, Jackson, MI. (ERIC Document Reproduction Service No. ED 340 546)

Many advising programs are not adequate because their environments are dominated by traditionalist attitudes rather than being consumer oriented. An overall academic advising evaluation procedure was developed including an adviser evaluation and an effective adviser assignment method. Many other aspects of the revised advising program are discussed. The appendices include the

forms used to implement the advisement
program.

327.   Kapraum, E.D., & Coldren, D.W.
(1980). An approach to the evaluation of
academic advising. Journal of College Student
Personnel, 21, 85-86.

An evaluation instrument to be used in
appraising the effectiveness of academic
advisers was developed by a subcommittee of a
faculty senate. The evaluation instrument is
designed to elicit a numerical rating of the
academic adviser in nine dimensions of
advising activities. These dimensions and the
program as a whole are discussed.

328.   Kelley, K.N., & Lynch, M.J. (1991).
Factors students use when evaluating advisors.
NACADA Journal, 11, 26-33.

Students' perceptions of advisers when
evaluating them were examined. A schematic
structure is devised which can be taken into
account when developing advising assessment
instruments. This research focused on how
students perceived and organized information
concerning adviser behavior.

329.   Kozloff, J. (1985). Delivering
academic advising: Who, what and how? NACADA
Journal, 5, 69-75.

In order to assess student needs and
perceptions of the advising process, a
questionnaire on academic advising was
administered. Student preferences were
investigated as indicators of what services
were most important to advisees. This article
suggests that important information on which
to base priorities may be best gained from the
student.

330.   Kozloff, J. (1987). A student-

centered approach to accountability and
assessment. Journal of College Student
Personnel, 28, 419-423.

The current management perspective in
assessing student outcomes can be redirected
so that assessment is used primarily to
promote student development and to enhance
learning. Any resulting program should be
sensitive to both personal and cognitive
development and should ensure that the results
of any programs that are used to enhance the
learning environment for students provide for
the development of faculty and student
talents, and answer public demands for
institutional accountability.

331.   Kramer, G.L. (1992). Using student
focus groups to evaluate academic support
services. NACADA Journal, 12, 38-41.

The use of student focus groups as an
evaluation method is examined in this article.
Student focus groups are perceptive and eager
to provide input. They provide a direct,
inexpensive, and effective research approach
that benefits the institution. Changes that
were made in various aspects of academic
support services as a result of student input
are described. Sample questions used in the
focus group are appended.

332.   Lecher, A. (1984). Academic
advisement center self-study report. (ERIC
Document Reproduction Service Report No.
ED 256 418)

A self-evaluation is provided of an advisement
center at a community college. Provided are
an overview of the center's history and
development, goals and objectives, the
instrument used to measure the programs's
effectiveness including external evaluations
and student evaluation, aspects of

student/program interaction, a review of
trends and issues related to student retention
and enrollment, the program's costs and
sources of support, relations with the off-
campus community, and the operations and
procedures designed to enhance program
cohesiveness.

333. Lunneborg, P.W., & Baker, E.C. (1986).
Advising undergraduates in psychology:
Exploring the neglected dimension. Teaching
of Psychology, 13, 181-185.

This article presents a brief description and
evaluation in departments of psychology based
on a national survey. The article notes that
the "all faculty" model of advising was most
popular and that the majority of institutions
provided no advising rewards or system for
evaluating advisers' performance.

334.   Neale, A., & Sidorenko, C. (1988).
Student evaluation: A model for improving
advising services.   NACADA Journal, 8, 72-82.

The rationale for implementing a student
evaluation of advising services was based on
the premise that for advising services to be
effective there must be evaluation. How can
advising services and adviser performance be
improved if students are not asked to rate
their experiences? This article explains the
methodology used in a computerized student
evaluation model that has been used for four
years, identifying the steps involved in
designing a questionnaire and in implementing
a student evaluation, and describes how
advising services and adviser performance can
be improved, based on student feedback.

335.   Patrick Henry Community College
academic advising program evaluation,
September 1, 1987. (1987). Martinsville, VA:
Patrick Henry Community College. (ERIC

Document Reproduction Service No. ED 303 177)
An evaluation of the college's academic
advisement program was undertaken to identify
problems and areas needing improvement.
Surveys were conducted for both adviser and
advisees to determine their perceptions of and
satisfaction with the advising process.
Various results from the students and advisers
are provided and discussed. In addition,
survey instruments and responses to open-ended
questions are appended.

336.   Ramos, B. (1993).   Evaluation,
recognition, and reward of academic advising.
In M.C. King (Ed.), New Directions for
Community Colleges, no. 82. (pp. 63-73). San
Francisco: Jossey-Bass.

This chapter examines the role of evaluation,
recognition and reward in the organization and
delivery of academic advising in the community
college. The value of establishing an
effective evaluation program is espoused. The
various elements to be considered in the
design and implementation of an evaluation
plan are described. An illustration of an
evaluation model at a community college is
given. The need and suggestions for
implementing a program to recognize and reward
good academic advising is provided.

337.   Russel, J.H., & Skinkle, R.R. (1990).
Evaluation of peer-adviser effectiveness.
Journal of College Student Development, 31,
388-394.

This study examines the results of a peer-
advising orientation program's impact on
participants' perceived and actual
involvement within the university and explores
peer advisers' characteristics. The results
indicate that the Peer-Advising Program had a
significant impact on the participants.
Students demonstrated a greater sense of

membership in the university community as well as more involvement in student activities than before the program.

338.   Sedlacek, W.E. (1987).   Evaluating student support services.   In J.F. Wergin and L.A. Braskamp (Eds.), Evaluating administrative services and programs.   New Directions for Institutional Research: Issue 56, Winter.

The purpose of this chapter is to present some ideas and approaches for evaluating support services.   Organizing the evaluation in terms of objectives, strategies, and measures is a useful beginning step.   Further categorization by traditional and nontraditional variables should help further specify the nature of evaluation.   Finally, attention to specific problems or models within this framework should enhance the thoroughness of an evaluation project.

339.   Srebnik, D.S. (1988).   Academic advising evaluation: A review of assessment instruments.   NACADA Journal, 8, 52-62.

In the interests of increasing the percentage of institutions that evaluate their advising programs and individual advisers, this study looks at survey instruments in four categories: those for students to evaluate advisers; those for students to evaluate advising centers; those with dual forms for advisers and students; and those given to advisers alone.   Surveys to advisers looked at advising rewards, attitudes towards advisers, advising objectives and advising resource usage.   Recommendations include greater use of either one survey or a combination, depending on the particular information sought, and commitment on the part of more institutions to conduct evaluations that will thoroughly point to advisers and program strengths and weaknesses in order to build improved advising programs.

340.   Vowell, F., & Karst, R. (1987). Students satisfied with faculty advising in an intrusive advising program. NACADA Journal, 7, 31-33.

The procedures involved in implementing an intrusive advising program is described. A questionnaire consisting of six questions was designed and administered by four trained, upperclass, paid interviewers from a random listing of students. The study successfully met its stated purpose of discovering the perceptions students held of advisers in the intrusive advising system.

341.   Wergin, J.F., & Braskamp, L.A. (Eds.)   (1987). Evaluating administrative services and programs. New Directions for Institutional Research: Issue 56, Winter.

This sourcebook deals with how universities and colleges can assess the effectiveness of their administrative support programs and services. The opening essay offers a general framework for evaluation, reviewing some successful models and strategies, and suggesting criteria for an evaluation plan. The other chapters look at the evaluation process in the context of specific functions and programs.

342.   Williams, E. (1992). Student attitudes towards approaches to learning and assessment. Assessment and Evaluation in Higher Education, 17, 45-58.

A study investigated the attitudes of first-year British college students toward peer and self-assessment and preferred teaching and learning approaches, including student-centered learning, teacher role, and

negotiation of assignments. Self-evaluation
was found to be more realistic than peer
evaluation. Students also preferred
guidelines for performance and assessment.

343.   Winston, R.B., & Sandor, J.A. (1984).
Developmental academic advising: What do
students want? NACADA Journal, 4, 5-13.

The Academic Advising Inventory was completed
by students in a variety of undergraduate
classes. The inventory included 22 pairs of
items representing developmental and
prescriptive advisee-adviser relationships.
The students' mean ratings indicated a
preference for the developmental over the
prescriptive item for 21 of the 22 pairs.
Other results are discussed.

Chapter 11

Academic Advising Books

344.   Frost, S.H. (1991). <u>Academic advising for student success: A system of shared responsibility.</u> ASHE-ERIC Higher Education Report No. 3. Washington, D.C.: The George Washington University.

This report focuses on outcomes of advising in the context of research on contact between faculty and students, students' involvement, and persistence. The information in this book is appropriate for those working to increase the positive outcomes of college through academic advising.

345.   Gordon, V.N. (1992). <u>Handbook of academic advising.</u> Westport, CT: Greenwood Press.

This book is intended to assist practitioners in the intricacies of advising students. It describes different organizational approaches for delivering advising services, outlines the basic tasks involved in the advising process, and summarizes advising approaches for the many special and diverse populations that advisers encounter. The vast wellspring of literature applying to academic advising from many disciplines is the foundation supporting the information imparted in this book.

346.   Grites, T.J. (1979). Academic
advising: Getting us through the eighties.
AAHE-ERIC Higher Education Research Report No.
7. Washington, D.C.: The George Washington
University.

This research report takes a comprehensive
look at the academic advising process.
Historical developments, delivery systems, and
interinstitutional interfacing of academic
advising are reviewed. Eight recommendations
for assessing advising programs are offered.

347.   Habley, W.R. (Ed.) (1988). The
status and future of academic advising -
problems and promise. Iowa City: The ACT
National Center for the Advancement of
Educational Practices.

This volume provides an in-depth look at
topics consistently viewed as critical to the
success of advising programs. In addition to
a summary of the Third ACT National Survey of
Academic Advising, there are chapters on such
topics as organizing advising services,
developmental advising, adviser training, and
evaluation. Exemplary advising programs are
also described.

348.   King, M.C. (Ed.) (1993). Academic
advising: Organizing and delivering services
for student success. New Directions for
Community Colleges, No. 82. San Francisco:
Jossey-Bass.

This volume views academic advising as the
only structured service on college campuses
that guarantees students' interaction with
concerned representatives of the insitutition.
It defines developmental advising, describes
the ways in which advising services are
organized and delivered, and discusses the key

components of effective advising programs.
Although geared to community colleges, much of
the information is relevant to other types of
institutions as well.

349.   Schein, H.K., Laff, N.S., & Allen,
D.R. (1987). Giving advice to students: A
road map for college professionals.
Alexandria, VA: American College Personnel
Association.

This book uses student needs as the basis for
cooperation between academic and student
affairs. Root concepts and critical thinking
skills which underlie all learning are
incorporated into a developmental advising
scheme. Five central elements of academic
advising are discussed: academic decision
making, resource identification and use,
career search, postgraduate studies, and
conseling.

350.   Winston, R.B., Jr., Ender, S.C., &
Miller, T.K. (Eds.) (1982). Developmental
approaches to academic advising. New
Directions for Student Services, No. 17.
San Francisco: Jossey-Bass.

Student development concepts are the focus for
detailing practical advising practices. The
academic advising process presents an
opportunity for incorporating student
development concepts beyond the realm of
traditional programing. An integrated
approach to educating students that addresses
personal as well as intellectual development
throughout the institution is espoused.

351.   Winston, R.B., Jr., Miller, T.K.,
Ender, S.C., & Grites, T.J. (Eds.) (1984).
Developmental academic advising. San
Francisco: Jossey-Bass.

This book provides a comprehensive examination

of academic advising from a developmental
perspective.   The seventeen chapters show how
advising programs can enhance the quality of
students' educational experiences, help them
adjust to the college environment, and help
them achieve educational, personal, and career
goals.   Responsible advising programs can also
further an institution's mission and goals and
decrease attrition resulting from a lack of
effective advising and mentoring.

Author Index

Numbers are citation entry numbers, not page numbers.

Silverman, T. 226
Skinkle, R.R. 70, 337
Sklare, L. 26
Sloan, P. 124
Smith, P.L. 162
Sobal, J. 36
Soo, J.K. 169
Sowa, C.J. 120
Spanard, J.M.A. 274
Spencer, R.W. 51, 55
Spicuzza, F.J. 13
Srebnik, D.S. 339
Stark, J.S. 307
Steele, G.E. 146, 155
Stewart, M.A. 162
Stewart, S.S. 125
Stokes, J.P. 27
Stott, F.W. 221
Subich, L.M. 228
Swanson, J.L. 249
Swift, J.S. 275

Tack, M.W. 134
Taylor, L.T. 87, 267
Teague, G.V. 28
Terenzini, P.T. 156
Terrell, P.S. 103
Theophilides, C. 156
Thomas, R.O. 75
Thompson, C.A. 104
Thompson, D.A. 269
Tinto, V. 276, 277
Tokar, D.M. 249
Trombley, T.B. 29
Tuttle, G.E. 9

Underwood, C. 121

Vickio, C.J. 134

Vincent, C. 71
Vohra, S. 71
Vowell, F. 30, 340

Wade, P. 128
Walker, S.P. 250
Wallace, G.R. 250
Wankat, P.C. 43
Weaver, F.S. 31
Wells, R.N. 185
Wergin, J.F. 341
Weston, P.K. 219
Wherly, B. 191
White, B. 224
White, E.R. 294
Whitely, S. 166
Wilder, J.R. 14, 251
Wilke, C.J. 104
Williams, E. 342
Wilmes, M.B. 124
Wilson, P.A. 123
Winston, R.B. 59, 72,
   91, 92, 93, 198,
   285, 343, 349, 350
Witten, C.H. 273
Wrenn, C.G. 305
Wright, B. 186
Wright, D.J. 164
Wyckoff, J. 268
Wysocki, J. 133

Yanez, M. 269
Yerian, J.M. 220
Young, D.P. 291, 292
Young, R.B. 306

Zimmerman, D.A. 67
Zingg, P.J. 122
Zultowski, W.H. 73

Subject Index

About the Compiler

VIRGINIA N. GORDON is Assistant Dean Emeritus at University College, The Ohio State University and is on the faculty in the College of Education. She is the author of many book chapters and journal articles and has published several books on academic and career advising, including *Handbook of Academic Advising* (Greenwood Press, 1992).